Nelson Byrd Woltz

GARDEN
PARK
COMMUNITY
FARM

Nelson Byrd Woltz

GARDEN
PARK
COMMUNITY
FARM

Warren T. Byrd Jr.
Thomas L. Woltz
Edited by Stephen Orr
Essays by Elizabeth Meyer

Princeton Architectural Press
New York

Published by
Princeton Architectural Press
37 East Seventh Street
New York, New York 10003

Visit our website at www.papress.com.

Editor: Sara E. Stemen
Designer: Jan Haux

Special thanks to: Sara Bader, Nicola Bednarek
Brower, Janet Behning, Fannie Bushin, Megan Carey,
Carina Cha, Andrea Chlad, Benjamin English, Russell
Fernandez, Will Foster, Diane Levinson, Jennifer Lippert,
Jacob Moore, Katharine Myers, Margaret Rogalski, Elana
Schlenker, Dan Simon, Andrew Stepanian, Paul Wagner,
and Joseph Weston of Princeton Architectural Press
—Kevin C. Lippert, publisher

Library of Congress Cataloging-in-Publication Data
Byrd, Warren T., Jr.
Nelson Byrd Woltz : garden, park, community, farm /
Warren T. Byrd, Jr., and Thomas L. Woltz ; edited by
Stephen Orr ; essays by Elizabeth Meyer. — First edition.
    pages cm
ISBN 978-1-61689-114-5 (hardcover : alk. paper)
1. Nelson Byrd Woltz Landscape Architects.
2. Landscape architecture — United States.
I. Woltz, Thomas L. II. Nelson Byrd Woltz Landscape
Architects. III. Title. IV. Title: Landscapes.
 SB470.53.B97 2013
 712.092—dc23
                            2012038800

pages 2–3
Dusk falls in Citygarden in St. Louis, Missouri, where
sculptures by Bernar Venet are dramatically illuminated
near a limestone arc wall forming the park's backbone.

pages 4–5
Dense plantings of herbs and vegetables thrive in a grid
of galvanized steel planters custom fabricated for the
Medlock Ames vineyards in Sonoma, California.

pages 6–7
Adjacent to the Pacific Ocean, the freshwater wetland
islands of Orongo Station in New Zealand feature a mix
of native hydric trees, shrubs, and marginal wetland
plants and serve as a safe habitat for flightless birds
during nesting season.

page 13
A perennial garden features plants originally collected
on the 1769 voyage during which Captain James Cook
discovered New Zealand.

Contents

Children play in the shallow water of the fountains at Citygarden in St. Louis. A waterfall cascades over rough, locally quarried stones, recalling the cliffs along the Mississippi River.

Natural Histories

Warren T. Byrd Jr.

I have loved being outside and drawing since I was very young; perhaps that is why my profession found its way to me. I remember keeping sketchbooks of birds and nests when I was nine years old. I do not know where my inclination to record natural phenomena came from, but I must give credit to that childhood endeavor. There, I found a kind of alchemy in how animals create their habitats in the natural context—I was moved to celebrate the outdoors, representing it on paper and later reimagining it in the built forms of landscape architecture.

Perhaps there is a certain providence attached to my family name—an affinity for creatures that fly and build nests in trees, among rocks, within marshes, and under eaves. I vividly remember discovering a red-eyed vireo's nest in my early teens and being fascinated with the way the bird had assembled its home out of both found objects and natural materials. I continue to be drawn to the imperfect beauty of these three-dimensional creations—constructions of tangential twigs woven into the forked branches of a tree or shrub, most often found in the margins of forests, fields, and streams.

Streams also played a primary role in my early appreciation of nature. Like many kids, I could not stay away from wet, muddy places teeming with life—the world of rocks and riffles, tadpoles and minnows, sewers and pipes, inlets and discharges. Deep pools shaded by arching trees with rope swings harbored turtles, frogs, and salamanders. The creeks offered muck and sand and whirlpools and runnels and rivulets and gentle falls and steep banks of ferns and prickers. Some part of the creeks—along with countless other bodies of water—remained with me. All those forms of water seeped into my bones and have, over the years that I have practiced as a landscape architect, leaked out in the form of the springs, basins, rills, and falls that I have designed.

An education in forestry, environmental conservation, horticulture, and then landscape architecture followed those teenage years immersed in natural history. After a few years of practice, I found a kindred spirit in someone who shared my nature-bound sensibility—my partner in life and work, Sue Nelson. Together we started a landscape-architecture office in 1985, collaborating on design projects of many scales throughout Virginia and the East Coast. We continue to enjoy life in the Virginia countryside with our daughter, Susanna.

This book is the fruit of thirty-five years of designing and creating landscapes. Teaching for more than twenty-five years at the University of Virginia has contributed deeply and directly to my design inclinations. What has kept me going is the simple realization that—like most landscape architects—I love what I do. This profession offers opportunities to let the mind and the pen wander while envisioning the possibilities of a piece of land. Landscape design demands a messy vitality because it is necessary to consider so many natural and cultural factors. And yet, working through many design layers, the landscape architect tries to create a clear diagram. No matter the complexity of the initial assignment, the best-designed places retain a simplicity of purpose and expression—they emphasize just a few salient qualities. Design evolves as an act of reclaiming, repairing, and recalling—never shying from a commitment to finding a deeper beauty in unexpected places and striving for a sustained resonance that floats between universal truths and the expressive details of a particular locale.

Certainly, landscape architecture is a profession, in the sense that the practitioner undergoes training, sits for licensing and certification exams, and stamps drawings to ensure health, safety, and welfare. But even more fundamentally, I see landscape architecture as a discipline within a wide-ranging field of study and practice encompassing everything from garden design to regional planning. Success in this field demands an extremely high level of proficiency, requiring discipline and preparation.

Preparation in design is about listening and learning. But when I started in school and in practice, it seemed that the field was taught as if intuition were everything. You often heard the truism that designers and artists are "born with it." So instruction tended to be fairly loose, relying primarily on the student to conjure ideas and develop designs out of pure imagination, or, if imagination failed, to merely copy historical examples. I felt that this was a questionable approach to teaching, learning, and designing because it did not create a distinct foundation for practice. As I taught and practiced more extensively, I immersed myself not only in landscape architecture but in the related design arts such as graphic design and architecture, and in the broader fine arts. I attempted to interpret the full spectrum of nineteenth- and twentieth-century cultural and academic "isms." Of particular fascination were the beaux-arts style, the Bauhaus, the garden-city movement, modernism, and early postmodernism. Was there any enlightenment to be found in deconstruction? What relationship was there to be found between modern practitioners and their notable predecessors?

The emphasis on precedents and typologies in the design world during the latter part of the twentieth century percolated through my thinking, teaching, and practice. My academic inquiry was augmented by considerable travel and the exploration of true masterworks of landscape architecture such as the Villa Gamberaia in Italy, Hestercombe in England, and the gardens of Kyoto, Japan. I would spend days feeling a landscape's proportions, scale, and sense of space, and how all these were affected by shifting light, air, scent, texture, color, and sound. Experiencing these iconic places provided an essential education. But after every trip, I always returned to the spartina marshes and meandering tidal creeks of the eastern shore of Maryland and Virginia. I revisited the fall-line crescendo of the great falls on the Potomac, or the forested world of black bears, timber rattlesnakes, rock ledges, outcrops, and slides in the Blue Ridge Mountains.

What has emerged is a set of design directions that correspond to many influences. The designed world is conceived in tandem with the natural world, recognizing that the most powerful places possess a magic born of peculiarities of region and time. These are landscapes that juxtapose human ideals such as rational geometric order with the natural circumstances of climate, landform, water flows, and plant communities. Landscape architecture is both a practical and an artful endeavor. It challenges you to embrace the tension between what is enduring and what is ephemeral. It asks you to find and make places that are centered, while simultaneously engaging the edges.

I believe in fundamental anthropological premises for the making of place, such as the prospect-refuge theory of human settlement and evolution (established by Jay Appleton in his influential book *The Experience of Landscape*). This notion that early peoples evolved within a savanna landscape suggests that humans have always sought protected, elevated edges between forests and clearings. These archetypal landscape associations constitute our deepest human-nature connections and seem to be wired into our collective memories. The best created landscapes take advantage of these primal associations to potently mesh the rational with the intuitive.

I credit a number of writers, from Henry David Thoreau to Wendell Berry, with guiding my course in these regards. I also acknowledge that my fundamental sensibility in landscape architectural practice originates with my parents, family, and teachers. This foundation has been continually reinforced and rekindled by student and professional friendships too numerous to recount, but certainly most fervently sustained by my long partnership with the ever-supportive, always articulate, and somehow tireless Thomas Woltz.

As you peruse these works, keep in mind that they were borne of a desire to affirm life and to assure healthy, vital environments. They reflect our deep and abiding collective desire to help preserve, protect, heal, and ennoble landscapes at all scales.

These projects and places were not created in a vacuum. They are not conceptions of a single mind but represent an extraordinary amount of collaboration and cooperation. We could not have achieved anything without the considerable contributions of colleagues in our two offices and the clients, contractors, craftsmen, and consultants who worked so closely with us over many years. This book speaks with the voices of many. For this we are forever grateful.

The reforestation of Orongo Station in New Zealand helps to protect the site's fragile clay soils from the severe erosion visible at the sea's edge; new plantings are protected from predators by six-foot-high steel fencing.

Path and Place

Thomas L. Woltz

Design is the physical expression of our intentions as individuals and as a society; these intentions have deeply personal roots that nurture and shape our positions in the world. This book project has been an opportunity to reflect on the major factors that have shaped me and that by extension now shape our practice. Three pivotal influences along my path toward landscape design stand out as the foundations of my current work: my childhood on a family farm, an extended period living overseas, and the design mentorship I experienced in my graduate education.

I grew up on the edge of a working cattle and crop farm belonging to my father's family in the Piedmont region of North Carolina, but it was observing and working with my parents in their backyard vegetable garden that most clearly demonstrated the links among food, the body, and the health of the land. My parents challenged themselves by growing everything they could to feed us year-round from terraced vegetable beds in the backyard. This annually consuming hobby began in late winter with flats of seeds sprouting in our sunny dining room and ended with the sweaty labor of August canning to preserve the vibrant bounty that would sustain us through the winter. The beginning of every meal was the pronouncement of when the bread was baked, when each vegetable was harvested, or some detail about its particular variety. Our chickens, compost, and soil were joined in an interdependent dance, the success or failure of each impacting the others.

The happy, small-scale stewardship involved in sustaining a family from the backyard stood in contrast to a larger, sadder story that unfolded on my mother's side of the family and which made an equal impact on my childhood imagination. My grandfather had managed his family's cattle farm in Haywood County, set among the magical mountains of western North Carolina. Known as Springdale Farm, the land was a portion of a large grant owned in the early 1700s by his ancestor Waightstill Avery, who gave it to his daughter and son-in-law, Selina Avery Lenoir and Thomas Lenoir. The farm was passed down through family until the onset of the Great Depression, when my grandfather was forced to sell this land after nearly two centuries of farming.

Interestingly, the farm was sold to Columbia University in New York City, where my great-uncle was the chair of botany. The farm was destined to become New College, an experimental agricultural-research station focused on sustainable farming and public education in the rural south. Though brilliant in its conception, New College was not long-lived, and the farm was later sold to developers who transformed the rolling fields and pastures into fairways and putting greens and the surrounding forest land into single-family development. The biodiversity of the forest and field mosaic gave way to suburban development patterns and a monoculture of water-hungry fescue. Perhaps I was comparing this to the richness of our small vegetable production in the backyard at home, but as we quietly drove past the simple neo-Grec wooden plantation house surrounded by tee boxes and golf flags, I knew that this was no longer a living landscape, as it once had been under the stewardship of my mother's family. Though a seed of awareness was planted at that time, I had no sense that my professional work might someday be spent in large part addressing these issues.

Years later, upon completion of a degree in architecture, I moved to Venice, Italy, where I worked for a contemporary-architecture practice that also specialized in historic restoration. It was there that I was instructed in the traditions of craftsmanship, materials, and scale in architectural design—all valuable lessons. But the greatest epiphany came in the form of an entirely new understanding of landscape. This unique Venetian environment consisted of nonliving elements: planes of patterned pavement, walls, expanses of water, dramatic variations of light, and other ephemera, including echo, reflection, and shadow. Like many people, I had always considered the landscape to be the forests, fields, parks, and gardens that had surrounded me all my life. I had a simple, horticultural awareness of landscape, and it was only after living for five years in a city that offered essentially none of these tropes that I realized that everything I experienced outside of buildings *was* the landscape.

It occurred to me that Venice's mineral, aqueous, and liminal landscapes could be the subject of design considerations every bit as rigorous as those I had naively reserved for architecture. Suddenly my definition of landscape expanded to a spatial language of abstraction, placemaking, and memory that was inclusive of horticulture but not limited to it. I returned to the United States to begin a master's degree in architecture at the University of Virginia and quickly applied to begin a second, simultaneous master's in landscape architecture to satisfy this curiosity.

This decision led to the third major influence on my design development: the faculty and design agenda of the UVA School of Architecture when I began my graduate studies in 1994. For a number of years, the faculty had been developing a keen interest and expertise in the arena of sustainability, and they had just selected as their new leader and spokesperson William McDonough, who would serve as dean during the years of my study. An emphasis on environmentally responsible design infused each department and classroom, and as I moved fluidly between classes in landscape and architecture, I began to realize that the two disciplines benefited from a close dialogue and that the scale of positive change achievable through landscape architecture was exhilarating.

I was fortunate to have Warren Byrd, former chair of the UVA Department of Landscape Architecture, as an instructor in horticulture, landscape design, and planting design. It was his mentorship that laid in my work the foundations of systems thinking, as well as a passion for design excellence and for plants and their native habitats. I also found the roots of my interest in narrative, design merged with science, and long-term land stewardship; now, sixteen years later, I am still guided by these important concepts.

These have become the hallmarks of what, years later, is Nelson Byrd Woltz, the practice we ran together as business partners for the last six years. NBW operates at the intersection of design excellence and ecological conservation to build a lasting relationship of stewardship toward the environments people inhabit. We believe in the power of design to shape communities positively, to reveal complex regional environments, and to restore disrupted ecologies. We use design to convey long-lasting stories of place: narratives of ecology.

Our design method begins with careful observation of a site and an intimate understanding of the proposed program and project goals. We map the tangible qualities and inherent energies beyond the ownership boundaries of the site, including prevailing winds, solar angles, hydrology, geology, and regional plant and animal communities, to provide a dynamic framework that often informs the primary design gesture. We understand that every site, whether an asphalt parking lot in New York City or a rain-forest fragment in New Zealand, has all of these embedded energies that inform our design process.

Early collaboration with a diverse range of professionals, including artists, scientists, craftspeople, historians, and engineers, helps us ask relevant questions of the site throughout the design process, questions that diffuse the boundaries of a typical practice. We draw from expertise inside and outside of the practice to tailor a critical kit of parts that responds to the program and belongs uniquely to the site at hand. These collaborations are at the heart of our practice and furnish important checks and balances against unintended consequences of design interventions.

Cultural research shapes our process as we seek to understand and record settlement and agricultural patterns, regional materials, and historic uses of a site. Often invisible, these traces and fragments can offer a rich foundation for contemporary design interventions. Historic tax maps, family letters of early settlers, archeological data, pollen spectrographs, and satellite photography are a few of the resources we have successfully used to unearth layers of use history and to shape a design.

During this research phase, we begin to formulate a narrative that will guide the process and inevitably be embedded in the resulting design. This concept of narrative, in which land is infused with stories waiting to be told, becomes the poetic structure of a design and the vehicle for a dialogue extending into the future between people and places. Often a narrative may be instrumental in shaping a design but is not necessarily interpreted in obvious ways for the public. Rather, subtly embedded information allows users to discover deeper layers not apparent at first glance.

A thoughtful position on horticulture leads us to evoke regionalism through the use of native plants or tell global stories through the juxtaposition of native and exotic plants. Plants are used for their cultural associations as much as for aesthetic, structural, and seasonal traits.

Geometry becomes a useful device for revealing distinctions between intervention and context, between flux and static, between design artifice and what may be perceived as natural. Through an iterative and collaborative design process of drawing, collage, and modeling, we develop multiple solutions that are edited into a final design to best meet the goals of the project and enhance the health of the site. Modernist design sensibilities and rigorous geometry form a frame for placemaking and restoration ecology at small and large landscape scales.

Innovations at NBW include broadening the traditional role of landscape architecture into the areas of restoration ecology, planning, civil engineering, horticultural design, and agriculture. Successful, perhaps unconventional design collaborations with sociologists, farmers, ornithologists, archeologists, and artists have brought added depth to design solutions across urban, rural, and historic sites. For example, the firm has worked to establish a high standard of aesthetic excellence in stormwater management and has encouraged a powerful expression of regionalism through the use of native plants and the protection of cultural landscapes in infrastructure projects. Our pioneering work in farmland conservation has drawn on our design expertise to interweave best practices of sustainable agriculture with rigorous restoration ecology for wetlands, forests, native grasslands, and wildlife infrastructure.

NBW hopes to encourage a responsiveness to the environment through artful designs and ecological narratives that connect people to place. Through this book, we hope to increase public understanding that the designed landscape is a powerful tool for implementing restoration ecology and for telling stories of the land that promote stewardship long into the future.

A vegetable garden structured by Cor-Ten steel at Iron Mountain House in Connecticut features a carved granite basin for washing vegetables.

PART I:
GARDEN
Sensing the Edge

Elizabeth Meyer

The possession of boundaries differentiates the garden from many other types of landscapes. A garden's edge delineates, encloses, and separates. But great garden edges are also places of encounter and negotiation, where differences between inside and outside can be brought into strong relief.

The experience of the garden's edge as a spatially and temporally prolonged encounter between here and there links NBW's gardens—despite extreme differences among their architectural settings, scales, and site geographies. Through their imaginative designs, NBW is giving shape to a new kind of garden—a hybrid of a classic walled garden, a minimalist garden without walls, and a profuse collection of plants.[1] One senses the edges of these gardens as exchanges as well as meditations on the relationship between home and the world. These connections are known through polysensual engagement—smelling, hearing, touching, tasting, and seeing while walking, gardening, playing, and moving.

From the early days of his university teaching career and the inception of his practice, Warren Byrd has been preoccupied with the garden as a space of experimentation, a receptacle of meaning, an index of place, and a source of sensory delight. Byrd's conviction that the garden was worth serious design consideration permeated the graduate design studios he taught and the firm he founded. In the sixteen years since Byrd and Thomas Woltz, one of Byrd's most accomplished students, began their professional collaboration, clients have brought a diverse array of garden-design challenges to the practice. Woltz's prior experience working as an architect in Italy introduced him to a design culture where the spatial and functional interconnections between architecture and gardens have a long tradition with contemporary implications. This expertise is evident in the firm's work; whether a house is one hundred years old or still on the drawing board, NBW shapes its spatial and topographic thresholds in unexpected and imaginative ways.

The principals of NBW know their medium—from the biology of how individual plants interact with soil, water, and climate to the landscape-ecosystem impacts of small design projects; from the textural qualities of particular species to the experiential potential of combining, layering, and massing varied plants; from the tectonics of an arbor to the proportions of a plinth. They ground garden-design speculations about the meaning of places in the material practices of planting, cultivating, and caring for plants; the cultural traditions of specific places; and the everyday lives of their clients. Byrd's and Woltz's interests in the garden as a vehicle for exploration, imagination, and provocation are extensions of their immersion in several worlds—the horticultural, the architectural, and the literary.

Top:
In a garden courtyard at Iron Mountain House in Connecticut, bluestone steps leading to a swimming pool cleave directly into the existing rock face.

Bottom:
Abundant perennial and shrub plantings transform the parking court of The Cedars, located on Long Island, New York, into a garden room of ever-changing seasonal interest.

1
Peter Walker and Cathy Deino coined the concept "minimalist gardens without walls" to describe tactics gleaned from contemporary art for creating landscape boundaries without enclosing vertical walls. See Mark Francis and Randolph Hester Jr., *The Meaning of Gardens: Idea, Place and Action* (Cambridge, MA: MIT Press, 1990), 120–29.

One can locate these characteristics in the plans, materials, planted-form typologies, and experiences of their realized garden commissions, as well as in Byrd's own words, written early in his teaching career.[2] One can seek and find meaning in NBW's serial explorations of garden edges and centers, figures and fields, enclosures and extensions—conditions understood as equivocal, ambiguous, and vacillating, never static. The spatial and material explorations of these edges and thresholds—some as small as a couple of steps, some forming complexly layered walls and hedges, and still others as large and immersive as a pine grove with a carpet of ferns—are where these gardens matter, where they are registered in experience: in the pause of the foot before descending a stair, the scent of a favorite blossom, the tactile quality of an ornamental grass, the taste of a ripe tomato. It is in the rediscovery of the spatial organization of the plan, and especially the invention within and along its edges, that NBW's gardens can be understood as places set apart from their context, yet inextricable from their settings.[3]

The three gardens selected for this monograph are variations on these themes. The Carnegie Hill garden fulfills a desire to occupy intimate inside-outside spaces on every inch of a small patch of urban ground and rooftop. The Iron Mountain garden satisfies a paradoxical vision to transform a degraded rocky outcrop into a rural retreat where rooms for gardening and play are slipped between jagged rock-face cliffs, sculptural fences, and minimalist concrete walls. The dozen or so garden rooms at The Cedars interact in a curious and satisfying scalar play; with the addition of carefully sited and calibrated terraces and nested garden enclosures, an existing country estate–era house is given a setting that reduces its apparent size, while greatly increasing its beauty and livability.

The Carnegie Hill garden in Manhattan's Upper East Side is a series of outdoor rooms that are spatial analogs and material interpretations of a bird's habitat. This analogy is apt, given the verticality of this narrow, multilevel urban residence. The edges of each garden are layered and composed of multiple materials. Enclosures made of layered wood, vines, and tree trunks wrap and weave around the edges of terraces. From the ground to the sky, they provide varied shelter and multiple comforts for a family. The thickness, the depth, the heights, and the flexibility of the material layers increase the performance of each garden room. Edges can be adjusted in response to the temperatures, light levels, and wind exposures of each side, affording privacy from adjacent buildings and setting up whimsical juxtapositions with nearby landmarks.

2
Warren T. Byrd, "Littoral Drifts: A Tidal Garden on the Eastern Shore of Virginia," *Modulus* 20 (1991): 130–39.

3
John Dixon Hunt, *Greater Perfections: The Practice of Garden Theory* (Philadelphia: University of Pennsylvania Press, 2000), 14–31.

The lowest and highest outdoor rooms offer lessons on how to create garden edges and layers that alter the perception of smallness to create an immersive landscape experience in the city. NBW understood that the best way to improve a small walled terrace on the ground level was to subdivide it two ways. The insertion of a spatial layer of tree canopies and trunks set six feet apart in the middle of the room makes the space seems larger. The layering changes the scale between elements and increases the perception of depth when viewed from the ground-floor kitchen. The second move responds to the double balcony that extends from the dining room on the floor above to overlook the ground-floor terrace. These two narrow, identical metal balconies deny the centrality or axiality of the garden, and suggested a diptych—two parts of radically different characters in dialogue with each other across a neutral center. One side of the ground-level terrace has a path to a white oversized marble basin that receives a wide sheet of water from a wide marble scupper. Its whiteness pulls light down into the garden, glowing against the green, vine-covered walls. The other half holds an oversized, circular woven seat lined with large pillows. This cozy spot is a favorite place for several members of the family to read to one another and to talk. Over time, as the vine scrim covers the three white walls, they and the ferns and other plantings on the ground plane will increasingly be perceived as a liner to the entire nestlike space. The garden habitat will be defined by unified vertical and horizontal surfaces of green permeated by sound, water, and light.

The upper, rooftop room is equally, if differently, layered. It exists in two parts, one lower than the other. Each level is partially enclosed by a high wall, one built of stucco and the other of grasses and multistemmed trees. The other sides vary in height, opening toward the southeast, the morning light, and the solitude of a church rooftop and steeple. These spaces are much smaller than the ground garden and could have felt inconsequential and exposed, given the vastness of the inner block of the city. But NBW understood the importance of high walls, not just for security from falls, but for scaling the gardens so that they felt protective and surreally intimate in contrast to the large water towers and apartment buildings nearby. They enclose and connect. In addition, the plants that compose the upper garden provide a microhabitat for migrating birds along the north–south flyway that passes over Manhattan. The Carnegie Hill garden is a place both set apart from and connected to its surroundings, through the layering of diverse performative materials and surfaces that shapes its edges and thresholds. It demonstrates what historian John Dixon Hunt identifies as the paradox of all great gardens—that they exist as *other* spaces, separate from the world, while simultaneously referring to their sites and milieus.[4]

The edge of the garden for Iron Mountain House in Connecticut is literally grounded in the rocky ledge of a site with a history of blasting. Retaining walls of stone and concrete connect and collide with the existing outcrops. The main rooms in the garden occupy this edge—a south-facing terrace off the living room of the house, a circular amphitheater of edible plants on the east, and a pool courtyard inserted between the guest house and the rock outcrop to the north. Like the Carnegie Hill garden, the center is less important than the edges that contain the social spaces of the garden and connect the house and garden to the surrounding matrix of meadows, pastures, and woods. The geography of the site establishes the geometries of the house and garden. Despite very different characters, compositional strategies, and material palettes, the Iron Mountain garden and the Carnegie Hill garden share a sensibility involving layered edges and thresholds, where built and planted forms overlap, weave, abut, collide, and unfold in unexpected, close proximity to each other. Both are family refuges, places simultaneously apart from their contexts yet connected to the world through a materially and experientially rich edge.

The Cedars is a built essay on edges at every scale—between house and garden, between garden room and garden room, between the site and its setting. These edges are richly sensory. Varied pavement materials register the character of each interior room—public, private, or service. Shady groves with duff floors afford privacy when one strolls along the boundary of the property or between garden rooms. Formerly barren pond edges are densely layered with wetland species to improve water quality and increase wildlife diversity. An earth berm along the western edge obscures adjacent suburban development but is notched at the center, registering the house axis and connecting the fields to a vestigial perimeter country lane that permits service-vehicles access to the fields and gardens.

NBW adapted tactics used by designers of great country-estate gardens, such as Edwin Lutyens, Gertrude Jekyll, and Beatrix Farrand, to address one problem of the existing house—its lack of transitions and connections to the large landscape. The first move NBW made was to create a terrace of varied dimensions around the house, defining its base. The designers shaped a series of small gardens and courts, one for each interior room of the house. These small spaces create interstitial edges between inside and outside that function as intimate extensions of the

4
Ibid., 14–15.

house. On the front, this terracing structures an entry and parking court, as well as a series of small gardens that direct and narrow one's gaze toward one bay of the house. It is a remarkable feat of scalar play; the quarter-acre forecourt introduces a new landscape scale to the site and, in doing so, makes the house more like a villa.

This tactic is supplemented by another strategy used on the western, rear side of the property, where an existing central axis, a two-acre pond, and a garden pavilion built and constructed by Chinese craftsmen would have perplexed most design consultants. But the resulting garden is, frankly, a masterwork of planted form and microtopography. NBW understood the importance of garden edges and layers in creating a series of discrete spaces and experiences with large transitional thresholds between them. This is achieved through the sophisticated spacing, layering, and combining of plants. The transitions between rooms are not made with banal, amorphous green masses that act as buffers. They are instead achieved through horizontally layered rows of native shrubs and familiar exotics (some left unpruned, others shaped into soft billows); through vertical strata of duff, ground cover, shrubs, and tree canopies that surprise with their weave of textures and scents; and through seasonal contrasts—the temporal and spatial figures of flowering understory drifts, fragrant bosques, and early- or persistent-fall-color-canopied clumps that emerge out of seemingly homogeneous woodlands.

The planted-form innovations in this garden remind me that Thomas Woltz has planted and cultivated a series of similar planted-form experiments on a smaller scale in his personal garden in Charlottesville, Virginia, for more than a decade. Unlike many landscape architects, he is a gardener as well as a designer. This experience gives NBW confidence and a sense of nuance in its use of planted form, whether designing transitional thresholds between geometric rooms or creating prominent foregrounds, where the character of a garden—its horticultural beauties—are given form.

Overleaf:
In Orongo Station Homestead's Earthworks Garden, a mounded collection of native hebes skirts the crisp lines of the architectural grading. The garden, framed by a circle of kauri (New Zealand's largest native tree), evokes the Maori tradition of earthworks.

Carnegie Hill House

Location: New York City
Site area: 979 square feet
Project dates: 2009–2010

At a townhouse on Manhattan's Upper East Side, NBW transformed each outdoor area—no matter how small—into a space designed for the full enjoyment of the home-owners and their young children. Surrounded by hectic city life, the four garden levels are inspired by the idea of a habitat, both in the sense of a nurturing retreat for the family and of a welcome stopover for regional bird and insect species. Consulting an ornithologist at the University of Maryland, the firm researched the types of birds that live in nearby Central Park and the habitats and botanical features that would be appealing to them. The needs of the visiting cast of house wrens, black-capped chickadees, and prothonotary warblers were considered while making a wide range of design choices: tree cover, seed sources, and specifications for nest boxes. Plant-ings can stand on their own as ornamental selections, but because they are so hospi-table to local and migratory bird species, they also enrich the owners' experience of the passing seasons and their accompanying wildlife.

To provide a haven for the resident family, a green ground-floor shade garden contains several living areas. Set among a line of 'Princeton Sentry' ginkgo trees, a large circular chair for reading or napping accommodates parents and children together. Instead of the traditional small city lawn, a compositional path of black locust sleepers steps through low-growing leucothoe, ostrich ferns, and lady ferns. These varieties, which had already existed on site, were stored during construction and later replanted. The straight ginkgo trunks frame views of both the nest chair and a white marble fountain as seen from the townhouse's large rear windows, creating a sense of depth and a strong diptych composition against the spare white stucco walls.

Small garden terraces are attached to rooms on the higher floors of the resi-dence. Rolling screens of slatted teak, crafted with a subtle pattern inspired by the interwoven construction of birds' nests, surround a children's teaching garden with a large slate blackboard. On the way up to the rooftop garden is a protected pocket playground, where a green wall contains hanging ferns, mint, and blue fanflowers in a seasonal display above a sandbox. Since the green wall sits directly above the chil-dren's sandbox, nontoxic plants were selected, in addition to edibles such as basil, rosemary, sage, thyme, and strawberries.

On the exposed seventh-floor level, a grove of birch trees and a sunny sky meadow of tall panicum and prairie dropseed grasses, baptisia, and other bird-friendly native species partially screen out neighboring buildings with their water towers and rooftop apparatus, while not rejecting the reality of being in the middle of New York City. Forestry Stewardship Council–certified teak screening and planters contribute to the sense of openness combined with privacy. Patterned bluestone paving echoes the roof tiles of an adjacent church. From top to bottom, the design celebrates the opportunity to bring biodiversity, microecology, and microclimates to an urban setting.

PRIMARY MATERIALS

Bluestone

FSC-certified teak

Living wall planting system

Slate

White marble

PLANTS

Upper Roof Terrace

Baptisia australis (wild blue indigo)

Betula nigra (river birch)

Calamagrostis stricta (slimstem reedgrass)

Gaura lindheimeri (white gaura)

Hydrangea arborescens 'Annabelle'

Lavandula (lavender)

Liatris spicata (blazing star)

Panicum virgatum (switchgrass)

Veronica longifolia (speedwell)

Lower Roof Terrace

Athyrium filix-femina (common lady fern)

Fragaria spp. (strawberry)

Gaultheria procumbens (Eastern teaberry)

Iberis sempervirens (candytuft)

Ocimum basilicum (basil)

Rosmarinus officinalis (rosemary)

Salvia officinalis (common sage)

Thymus vulgaris (thyme)

Children's Terrace

Adiantum tenerum (maidenhair fern)

Allium 'Globemaster'

Buxus 'Green Velvet' ('Green Velvet' boxwood)

Phlox divaricata 'Blue Perfume' (woodland phlox)

Ground Floor

Anemone 'Honorine Jobert' (Japanese
     anemone)

Astilbe chinensis 'Finale'

Galanthus nivalis (snowdrop)

Ginkgo biloba 'Princeton Sentry'

Matteuccia struthiopteris (ostrich fern)

Ophiopogon japonicus (mondo grass)

Parthenocissus tricuspidata (Boston ivy)

Polygonatum odoratum (Solomon's-seal)

Prunus laurocerasus 'Otto Luyken'
     ('Otto Luyken' English laurel)

Scilla siberica 'Spring Beauty'

Tiarella 'Spring Symphony' ('Spring
     Symphony' foamflower)

Vinca minor (dwarf periwinkle)

In the sky meadow on the seventh floor of
Carnegie Hill House, a row of multistemmed
river birch underplanted with native grasses
and wildflowers partially screens the view
of adjacent towers and rooftop water tanks
with leaves and branches.

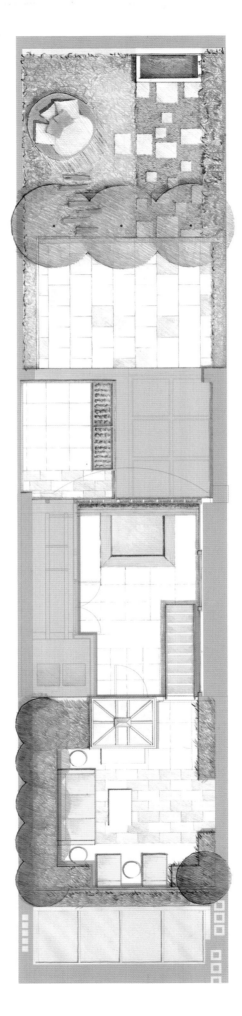

Left:
Plan of gardens at Carnegie Hill House

Opposite:
A living wall of herbs, berries, annuals, and perennials functions as a work of art and as the backdrop for children's play in a sunken sandbox. Woodwork crafted from Western red cedar will be allowed to age naturally.

Top:
Custom-built wooden screens can be
closed to create a private courtyard or
opened to frame a remarkable view of the
spire of a nearby church. NBW handled
all the design details for these spaces,
including handrails, stair treads, and paving.

Bottom:
The uppermost terrace's sky meadow
enhances the view of the diverse cityscape
surrounding the site and provides a winter
nesting habitat for birds.

Opposite:
The top-floor garden features pockets of
casual seating surrounded by lush native
warm-season meadow grasses and
perennials.

Right:
Western red cedar slats surround a
chalkboard on the west wall of the children's
terrace.

Opposite top:
A balcony off the formal dining room
overlooks a diptych garden with seating and
fountain areas. Stainless-steel cables form
a trellis for hops that will grow against the
garden's rear wall.

Opposite bottom:
Under the cool shade of ginkgoes, locust
logs embedded in groundcover evoke a
woodland setting.

Overleaf:
Ginkgo trees create a sense of depth and
serve as a filigree screen between a dining
terrace and the small garden.

The Cedars

Location: Long Island, New York
Site area: 27 acres
Project dates: 2005–2010

On the low, flat plains of the north shore of Long Island, an early twentieth-century French Norman–style manor house sits on one of the few remaining intact estates of the Gilded Age. When new owners arrived, the landscaping consisted of a few grand but aging vestiges of a 1920s garden. Given the vast scale of the space, NBW conceived of an overarching design theme: the contemporary estate as a botanic garden housing all the necessary elements of modern life for the new homeowners, an active young family.

The husband and wife were deeply committed to returning the estate to its historic heyday. The firm kept existing walled gardens and introduced an expanded program of new garden areas just around the house that match its scale and architectural quality. But NBW also required a design concept that would help them make plant selections throughout the many acres of the property and establish a clear narrative of horticulture. The property was therefore divided—in spirit more than physically—into three long, narrow zones; these delineations guided the organization of elements and species according to their cultural associations and natural history.

Each zone represents ideas borrowed from one of three geographic regions located along the thirty-eighth parallel—the same latitude as the property. The first zone takes its cues from the North American emphasis on the body, outdoor activity, and sports. Here are tennis courts (designed to look more like garden rooms, with elegant painted-wood fencing); a swimming pool; and a walled vegetable garden. The plant palette includes primarily North American species. A central zone directly behind the house is a celebration of the mind and of the Cartesian geometry of classic Western European garden design, with a double allée of pollarded planetrees that extends from the axis of the house. These allées flank a central lawn and an eighty-foot-long rectangular water basin with pencil jets of water. The third zone, based on ideas relating to the spirit, displays the influence of Asian elements of borrowed scenery, meandering paths, and a sense of enclosure. A strategy of hide-and-reveal is evident in a secret walled garden and in sinuous paths that wind through a tall woodland of maple and pine trees and Asian plants such as Japanese maples and cryptomeria.

Another organizing scheme, this one oriented from the front entrance to the back of the property, was laid over these three zones. The front third of the site was reconceived as a private arboretum. An original straight axial drive that ran directly to the front of the house was reworked into a series of gentle curves through a woodland garden planted with native beech, oak, and hemlock and an understory of rhododendrons. The middle section surrounds the house on all sides with a collection of primarily flowering garden plants arranged in classic garden rooms, each accessible from an interior room of the house through wide doorways. The back third calls upon the

PRIMARY MATERIALS

Blue painted gates and fences

Fired bronze chain

Old Virginia brick

Western red cedar

PLANTS

Front of property

Aesculus parviflora (bottlebrush buckeye)

Fagus grandifolia (American beech)

Hydrangea quercifolia (oakleaf hydrangea)

Nyssa sylvatica (black gum)

Rhododendron catawbiense 'English Roseum'

Rhododendron vaseyi (pinkshell azalea)

Viburnum spp. (arrowwood)

Gardens near house

Amsonia hubrichtii (threadleaf bluestar)

Cotinus coggygria 'Royal Purple' ('Royal Purple' smoketree)

Platanus occidentalis (American planetree)

Prunus x *yedoensis* (Yoshino cherry)

Thuja occidentalis (American arborvitae)

Vitex agnus-castus (chaste tree)

Forest/Pine grove

Dennstaedtia punctilobula (hayscented fern)

Kalmia latifolia (mountain laurel)

Picea abies (Norway spruce)

Pond

Acer rubrum (red maple)

Clethra alnifolia (summersweet)

Hamamelis virginiana (American witchhazel)

Brick-lined paths of decomposed granite meander through the woodland fern garden at The Cedars.

agricultural history of the site and the open feeling of planted fields, with a wildflower meadow, a cutting garden, and an additional vegetable garden.

The design vocabulary of the garden takes traditional hardscape elements such as parterres, axes, paving patterns, and allées and updates them in a contemporary language of clean lines and unexpected treatments of materials; this carries the garden through all four seasons within a strong visual framework. Ever-changing spectacle differentiates the seasons: ten thousand white daffodils bloom under the planetrees in spring, and long rows of Yoshino cherry trees burst into flower in the spring, give shade in the summer, and burn crimson in the fall over a sea of bright yellow amsonia.

Even with multiple systems of conceptual divisions, the vast garden feels harmonious. Intimate garden rooms juxtaposed with long vistas provide interest and a human scale for the otherwise flat topography with its lack of dramatic grade change. The firm's primary concern was to transform a monoculture of large amounts of turf grass and evergreens by adding hundreds of additional species. NBW thus established a biodiversity rarely seen in a formal garden in a suburban setting, benefitting the homeowners and local wildlife alike.

Top:
Cedar trellises provide structure for bramble fruits and climbers while dividing garden areas in a walled potager. Custom-designed blue gates are a signature of The Cedars.

Bottom:
The walled potager, which features large-scale cedar tomato towers, is a display of summer exuberance matched with utility.

Opposite top:
Limestone piers, fieldstone walls designed to frame and anchor the pool area, and sheared English yew hedges create a sense of enclosure. Minimal paving allows the space to feel more like a garden than the typical setting for a swimming pool; two bosques of littleleaf lindens visible beyond the enclosure form a threshold to distant playfields.

Opposite bottom:
The Cedars master plan

Overleaf:
A spring display of white narcissus planted under twin allées of pollarded sycamore trees flank an eighty-foot-long reflecting pool.

Top:
Stonework piers hung with bronze chain create a loose sense of enclosure in the parking court garden, where a large panel of grass is stabilized to support cars. Abundant plantings mitigate the utilitarian functionality of a typical parking area and transform it into an important garden room.

Bottom:
Hand-crafted paving of thin bluestone turned on end creates a rich surface texture in the entry-hall court.

Opposite:
A formal reflecting pool is a visual echo of a more naturalistic two-acre pond in the distance.

Top:
Spring bloom dominates the cherry allée in March. When the perennial amsonia plantings are dormant during early spring and winter, massive pots visually punctuate the long walkway.

Bottom:
In fall the cherry allée is transformed in a brilliant display of autumnal foliage. Pots are filled with plants, as the space is seasonally transformed by the vivid yellow color of amsonia.

Opposite:
The breakfast terrace's irregular paving allows plantings such as lady's mantle to spill in from the adjacent borders. Stones have been removed in multiple locations to allow more space for fragrant herbs and flowering perennials.

Right:
A pondside pavilion was designed and constructed by craftsmen from China. It is surrounded by marginal wetland native plants, providing a vantage point of the abundant wildlife nestled in the island's plantings.

Opposite top:
NBW designed arching bridges with a contemporary interpretation of design details found in the Chinese pavilion to access the pond's two islands, where densely planted perennials and shrubs create an immersive horticultural experience.

Opposite bottom:
Long views across the pond reveal a shoreline that is edged with bold stands of plants to prevent erosion and to create habitats for amphibians and birds.

Overleaf:
A grove of saucer magnolias flanks one of the curved bridges. Wooden rails echo the form of the bridge's visible steel frame.

Iron Mountain House

Location: Northwestern Connecticut
Site area: 300 acres
Project dates: 1999–2006

Rough stone cliffs, rich with golden-brown tones and bands of oxidized iron, provide the color palette for this series of garden spaces surrounding the contemporary house of an art collector on a three-hundred-acre working farm. NBW integrated the house into its dramatically rugged cliffside setting by conceiving of the garden's creation as if it had been scooped, quarrylike, from the blasted, forest-ringed cliff. By highlighting rather than ignoring the nineteenth-century regional history of iron-ore mining at the site, the domestic architecture is peacefully assimilated into its incongruous surroundings by the careful weaving in of natural elements and plants.

Large retaining walls built of stone that resembles the cliff face and board-formed concrete relate respectfully to the angular, abstract forms of the house; together, they create two courtyards. Additional long, smooth walls further delineate the spaces and hurtle into the rough face of the hillside on the back side of the house. Two garden rooms, lush with perennial and woodland plants, contain the only small lawns on the property. They are linked to the front of the house by a continuous ribbon of cut-flower borders of native species and grasses that runs around the back and then along the top of the retaining walls above the meadow. Behind the courtyards, separated from them by a low wall of board-formed concrete, is a terrace of low grasses. The low walls run directly into the rock face, acting as a reminder of the blasting, excavation, and piling of stone that created the rear threshold to the house; in addition, they divide the larger landscape of the entry court from the more intimate family gardens, which are meant to be appreciated from inside the house as well as experienced directly. The north-south walls are fieldstone, while those running east to west are made of concrete.

Sunken between the main level of the house and the rear cliff is the property's biggest surprise—a vegetable garden constructed as a terraced theater. This half-circle formed of three tiers of edible plants takes a common garden feature that has historically been a hidden working area and puts it directly at center stage. Low, half-inch-thick Cor-Ten steel retaining walls were fabricated locally and echo sculptures on the property made of the same material. These expressive shapes delineate the planting areas between the retaining walls, while creating staggered flights of gravel-filled steps that lead to a small circle of clipped grass and a gate to the meadow and surrounding forest. In winter, the space retains its sculptural quality even when devoid of seasonal crops.

On the other side of the house, stairs formed of cut slabs of bluestone lead up to a swimming pool designed by Gund Partnership to be reminiscent of a flooded quarry that is wedged into the blasted rock face. NBW tempered the stony setting with a collection of primary-succession plants—species such as staghorn sumac and serviceberry that would be the first to populate a disturbed mining site. These were

PRIMARY MATERIALS

Board-formed concrete

Connecticut fieldstone

Cor-Ten steel

PLANTS

Actaea racemosa (bugbane)

Agastache 'Blue Fortune' (anise hyssop)

Amelanchier lamarckii (serviceberry)

Cladrastris kentukea (American yellowwood)

Comptonia peregrina (Sweet-fern)

Cornus sericea (red twig dogwood)

Crataegus viridis 'Winter King' ('Winter King' hawthorn)

Dennstaedtia punctilobula (hayscented fern)

Echinacea purpurea (purple coneflower)

Eupatorium maculatum (joe-pye weed)

Fothergilla major 'Mt. Airy'

Monarda didyma (bee balm)

Panicum virgatum 'Haense Herms' (red switchgrass)

Schizachyrium scoparium (little bluestem)

Thalictrum rochebrunianum (meadow rue)

Board-formed concrete walls are poured to engage directly with natural rock outcroppings.

installed in pockets of imported soil among planted bioswales that direct sediment-loaded stormwater away from the swimming area.

Above the stone walls and meadows, the house's large windows afford views of the unspoiled valley and mountains beyond. A series of linked simple stone terraces with outdoor furniture and narrow beds run along the top of the tall retaining walls, which project into the three-acre native-grass and wildflower meadow. The firm converted high-maintenance mown fescue turf to meadow in a collaboration with meadow expert Larry Weaner. The plant palette of the beds is composed of grasses and cultivars of native regional wildflowers, including penstemons, veronica, veronicastrum, echinacea, and monarda. The beds peak in late summer and add a visual and horticultural link to those species found in the less cultivated, vast, open hillside below, with its system of walking trails designed to connect various parts of the farm.

Top:
Views across amphitheater and courtyards
and through a *porte-cochère* link inner and
outer garden areas.

Bottom:
Plan of Iron Mountain House

Opposite:
A long view framed by trees and the
architecture of the house guides the eye
over the meadow to the woods beyond. The
design for the courtyards that form the living
spaces for the family and pets becomes the
primary organizing spatial element of the
domestic complex in a setting that is at once
cultivated and wild.

Overleaf:
Poured-in-place concrete walls and jagged
rock faces stitch the site's built structural
elements into the existing landscape.

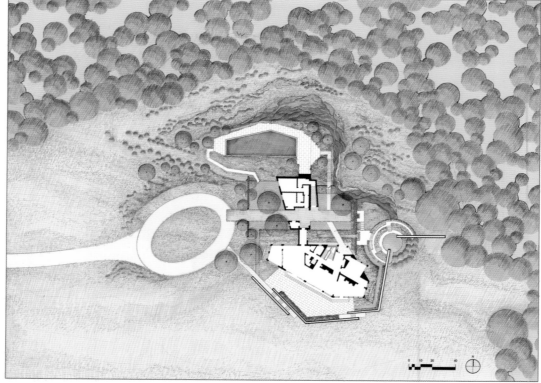

Top:
The pool garden overlooking the house and courtyard suggests a quarry swimming hole. Around the pool, designed by Gund Partnership, NBW added a native palette of first-succession species in small pockets of soil in the surrounding rock faces.

Bottom:
The cultivated garden areas butt into the jagged natural rock face of the site in surprising but satisfying ways.

Opposite:
The massive stone walls sheltering the plantings within the Cor-Ten vegetable amphitheater support a higher base for the house as well as a pathway for strolling its perimeter.

Left:
Carefully designed plantings of grasses and native meadow plants create a dramatic and seasonally varied arrival sequence for the homeowner.

Opposite top:
A Cor-Ten fence is designed to meet swimming-pool codes while evoking the patterns of the white birch trunks in surrounding woodlands.

Opposite bottom:
Wildflowers bloom in the meadow, which is mown only twice a year.

Top:
Massive stone walls create a dramatic
boundary between the garden areas near
the house and the wildflower meadow
below. Cultivars of native wildflowers
are used in the terrace gardens, while
unhybridized forms of the same species
thrive in the wilder areas.

Bottom:
Wildflower and warm-season grass-
meadow ecology can be maintained
by controlled burning once every three
years or by mowing once a season.
Both management methods offer greatly
reduced maintenance schedules.

Opposite top:
Snowfall reveals the crisp geometric
structure of the steel bands of the
vegetable garden, in contrast to the
lush foliage of summer months.

Opposite bottom:
Visitors to the house pass through a series
of layered landscapes, from woodland
to wildflower meadow to arrival garden,
through a *porte-cochère* and back to the
woodlands beyond.

Overleaf:
The prow of the massive fieldstone retaining
walls offers long views over the meadow to
a twenty-acre lake and woodlands beyond.

PART II:
PARK
Extraordinary Affects and Effects

Elizabeth Meyer

Public parks come in all sorts, sizes, and sites. NBW's range of park designs is as varied as it gets—a playful sculpture park in downtown St. Louis, Missouri; a somber memorial park in rural Pennsylvania; and a surreal zoological park in Washington, DC. Like most memorable parks, Citygarden, the Flight 93 memorial, and the National Zoo Asia Trail are more than patches of lawn and trees. They are important social spaces and cultural institutions. They are places of encounter with others, whether human or nonhuman, living or dead.

In public parks, these encounters are often experienced while moving through spaces combining designed and found nature. In 1868 Frederick Law Olmsted best explained the rationale for such activity when he told the Prospect Park Scientific Association, "A park is a work of art, designed to produce certain effects upon the minds of men."[1]

Olmsted's statement might surprise many contemporary designers and urban dwellers who think of parks as nothing more than free and open greenswards. But it was not lost on architecture critic Sarah Goldhagen.[2] In her essay "Park Here," which focused on significant new urban parks including NBW's Citygarden, Goldhagen outlined the characteristics of a park as a truly public place, where people not only gather but develop a sense of what they hold in common as a community. One of her criteria expands on Olmsted's definition: the experience of a park should offer the "possibility of a transformational personal experience in the city."[3] NBW designed each of the parks described in this section with the construction of experience in mind. The design of spatial sequences, as well as the detailing of walls, pavement, and seating, were considered in terms of their effects on park visitors and zoo animals.

Goldhagen's other criteria for a successful park are also germane to our appreciation of NBW's work. She calls for parks that possess "aesthetic coherence" and a "deep narrative richly told" as designed forms and spaces; the associations they evoke are key prompts for the construction of experience, the park's affective power.[4] Byrd and Woltz frequently deploy narrative in their projects as a tool for imbuing meaning. These narratives are not explicitly iconographic; rather they seek to connect a park to a larger landscape reference—the region or site beyond the parcel, or the role of nature or ecological processes within a particular city. So the use of a certain plant palette at the Flight 93 memorial park alludes to the time of year when Flight 93 crashed on September 11, 2001. For instance, red maples are resilient primary-succession species that are bright red when in fall leaf, as well as in their late-winter to early-spring bloom. The alignment of the entrance

Opposite:
An overview of Citygarden in St. Louis, Missouri, reveals its major structural elements: mounds and grade changes, plazas, arced walls, strolling gardens, and groves of native trees.

1
Charles E. Beveridge and Carolyn F. Hoffman, *The Papers of Frederick Law Olmsted. Supplemental Series, Volume 1: Writings on Public Spaces, Parkways, and Park Systems* (Baltimore: Johns Hopkins University Press, 1997), 155.

2
Sarah Goldhagen, "Park Here," *The New Republic*, September 2, 2010, 20–25.

3
Ibid., 22.

4
Ibid., 22ff.

wall traces the final approach of the plane. These spatial alignments, color choices, and temporal cues reinforce a sense of place, increasing the personal connections among visitors and the people and events memorialized.

At Citygarden, narrative takes shape through the juxtaposition of two different natures or landscapes. The first is derived from the great limestone river bluffs and river meanders that characterize the Mississippi and Missouri river valleys. The forms and materials of the two long lines that define the park, one for interacting with water and one for sitting, are transposed from these distant but well-known regional landscapes. The second is an erased landscape—the former building lots and alleys that once crossed and filled the Citygarden site. This smaller grain establishes the location of paths and gardens within Citygarden. It is not necessary to know either of these references in order to enjoy the park, but interaction and events in the park occur within and along walls, seats, and walks that are organized according to this narrative structure. The rhythms of everyday life in the park occur within beats, gestures, and alignments that were gleaned from the larger bioregion.

I wonder about the effects of these enclosures and surfaces on the racially diverse families that gather at Citygarden in hot weather to play among sculpture in the extensive waterfalls, jets, and pools. St. Louis's residential neighborhoods are dispersed and located far from the park. Most families would need to drive or take public transit to Citygarden. Do they find community in their shared humanity—seeking spaces to play in the cool microclimate of the park? Might the larger contextual references remind them they share a home—the city and the regional landscape—despite their differences? These are questions that all parks raise, often unanswered. It is the reason Goldhagen found Citygarden so compelling. In its formal and social spaces, Citygarden is more than beautiful, well made, comfortable, and free. NBW aimed to create park experiences that might gather strangers together. Community is built on nothing less.

The Asia Trail is part of a much larger zoological park located within Rock Creek Park in Washington, DC. Designed by Olmsted's firm in the late nineteenth century, the institution has since struggled with the tension between its park setting and the zoo's research and display mission. Within the five-acre Asia Trail, a visitor's experience is radically different than that found in other sections of the National Zoo. That tension is resolved through the design of an otherworldy new space where humans and animals encounter one another. The thick, spatial layers of ashlar stone and gabion walls, rock outcrops, bamboo scrims and arbors, metal railings, and plants that define the path appear to connect people to animals as much as separate them. The edges of the path are densely programmed and delineated, widening to become a small amphitheater, narrowing to slim thresholds, rising and falling to alter the relationship between human and nonhuman habitats. This affiliation between humans and animals through shared enclosures, novel assemblies of materials, and unexpected viewing configurations is amplified by the sharing of constructed microclimates. Machine-made mist and fog hover over both animal enclosures and viewing areas, improving the comfort of both zoo residents and visitors during Washington's brutally hot summer weather. Here, as in NBW's other parks, the experience of moving through the designed landscape alters one's psychological state as well as one's perceived relationship to others and to the environment. But at the National Zoological Park, that changing relationship to others can be surprisingly re-centering. As zoos question the balance between entertainment, recreation, and research, what is the role of animal display? What is the import of producing "certain effects" in the minds of the men, women, and children who visit Asian species of animals under a cool, misty fog, beneath a scorching summer sky?

The parks designed by NBW for commemoration, recreation, entertainment, and education challenge preconceptions and foster new perceptions about the meaning of human relationships to one another and with the biophysical world. While these parks integrate best practices for sustainable landscapes, they do so much more. They tell stories through the assembly of landscape. These parks cannot be confused with found nature; there is too much evidence of the designer's hand. For this reason, Goldhagen criticizes Citygarden for being, perhaps, overdesigned in parts. Perhaps.

But recent research offers another lens for considering the apprehension of an artist's hand and the resulting aesthetic sensations. Art historian David Freedberg and neuroscientist Vittorio Gallese posit that the "vigorous handling of the medium" in a work results in an empathetic aesthetic response on the part of the observer. Or, in other words, "The visible traces of the artist's creative gestures, such as vigorous modeling in clay and paint, fast brushwork and signs of the movement of the hand" produce a somatic response in the body and in the mind. They speculate that this response is "neuroesthetic" and is independent of cultural or historical references.[5]

This research opens up tantalizing implications for architecture and landscape architecture. If their findings can be applied not only to art objects but

5
David Freedberg and Vittorio Gallese, "Motion, Emotion, and Empathy in Esthetic Experience," in Mark Foster Gage, *Aesthetic Theory: Essential Texts for Architecture and Design* (New York: W. W. Norton, 2011), 309–23.

also to spatial works of art such as buildings and landscapes, then evidence of the landscape architect's hand might result in an empathetic aesthetic response that has a neurological basis. This neuroesthetic empathy with a designed space might prove deeper than a response based solely on natural aesthetics, the result of human interaction with found nature. The park designs of NBW, in their aesthetic coherence and narrative structure richly told through palpable design tactics and material assemblies, might offer new effects on the minds of men, women, and children and new "transformational personal experiences" through human relationships with other species that share our environment.

Opposite top:
The fountain plaza at Citygarden has 102 water jets that can be programmed for various lighting and water effects.

Opposite bottom:
An NBW-designed bridge crosses over animal habitats and offers sweeping views of the Asia Trail and its animal inhabitants at the National Zoo in Washington, DC.

Overleaf:
Citygarden's steps and accessible ramps are artfully composed and function as impromptu seating for people watching.

Asia Trail at the Smithsonian National Zoological Park

Location: Washington, DC
Site area: 5 acres / 480,000 square feet
Project dates: 2001–2007

Folded into a steeply sloping site in Rock Creek Park is a narrow five-acre section of the National Zoo dedicated to the health and well-being of seven types of endangered Asian animals: sloth bears, clouded leopards, fishing cats, Asian otters, a giant salamander, red pandas, and the iconic and much-beloved giant pandas. For the transformation of this underused area, NBW worked with zoo officials to identify the habitat requirements of these varied creatures while also considering the needs of more than one million human visitors a year, all eager to catch at least a glimpse of these rare species.

While striving to be as animal-friendly as possible, the designers also acknowledged that we don't live in the unspoiled world where these animals once thrived in isolation. Often even in the wild, these species live in altered environments, in ever-greater proximity to humans. The key to the design of the Asia Trail was in thinking not just of how humans could enter an animal environment but of how animals could thrive in a human environment. To reinforce the idea of coexistence, the design included interpretations of village settings and construction details inspired by the local customs of the species' home territories, to recreate the close link that humans and animals share in Asia.

The desire was foremost to separate the animals safely from visitors without unduly constricting them. This was accomplished by recreating features of their homelands while blurring the edges of the enclosures so that boundaries were impassable but not always evident to the casual observer. Plates of glass or woven wire nets create nearly invisible barriers and alter the perception of captivity. Rocky cliffs and ledges repeat throughout the trail, and visitors would be hard-pressed to identify which installations are actual stone and which are fabricated to accommodate the animals' needs.

Multiple routes created from permeable resin-based paths wind sinuously through the project. Some swoop above stormwater-capturing ponds that mimic forested native pools and streams. Others lead down into the lowest part of a thirty-to-forty-foot drop that is situated off the main, curving Frederick Law Olmsted–designed path through the zoo's other sections. Visitors are immersed in a complete sensory experience along with the animals; on Washington's hot, humid summer days, misters spray clouds of cooling fog over pathways just as they do in the animal habitats. Green roofs cover the buildings inside the exhibit, helping alleviate runoff and also concealing building materials. The regimen involved in handling and separating the three kinds of water systems on the project (stormwater, human, and animal) proved to be a challenge. Stormwater can be filtered in bioswales and reused, but any other water that enters or exits an animal's habitat must be sent through its own treatment system so that no runoff goes into the general system or into another animal's enclosure, to prevent the spread of animal diseases and pathogens.

PRIMARY MATERIALS

Bamboo and steel structures

Cor-Ten steel railings

Gabion walls

Ipe wood decking

Local stone for walls and boulders

Resin-based paving

Stabilized crushed stone paving

Steel mesh

Steel structures

PLANTS

Acer griseum (paperbark maple)

Acer rubrum (red maple)

Anemone x *hybrida* (Japanese anemone)

Callicarpa americana (American beautyberry)

Davidia involucrata (dove tree)

Dianthus spp. (dianthus)

Prunus spp. (cherry)

Quercus phellos (willow oak)

Rhododendron spp.

Rhus spp. (sumac)

Salix spp. (willows)

Sedum spp.

Various bamboo species

Viburnum spp.

Large stone outcrops offer basking areas for the giant pandas that encourage charismatic behavior for visitors yet also provide retreats from public view. Some stones are outfitted with coils of chilled water to cool the animals in the summertime heat of Washington, DC.

A primary challenge of this project was finding a suitably exotic but environmentally responsible way to recreate nature on the margin between the Piedmont and coastal plain regions surrounding Washington, DC. To accomplish this, NBW used vicariad species (related species that occur naturally along the same latitude in both Asia and in North America). These included foreign species of rhododendrons, amelanchier, and magnolia along with native versions of the same genera, which were added to the existing tree canopy of oak, hickory, maple, and tulip trees. All through the evocative space can be found the signature plant of Southeast Asia: quick-growing but retained bamboo, used as green walls, dividers, screens, drifts, archways, and groundcover.

The project was an intensive learning process for NBW, who relied heavily on the zoo staff and the expertise of special consultants to learn as much as possible about the seven animal species and their needs. They visited and studied like-minded innovative facilities such as the Bronx Zoo in New York City and Woodland Park Zoo in Seattle, which are known for their animalcentric approaches. The result is a transformative journey that starts as soon as a visitor steps off the wide asphalt path through the conventional areas of the zoo and enters the bamboo-lined trail with its rare, often-secretive inhabitants.

Top:
An amphitheater for viewing sloth bears is built of fieldstone and incorporates large outcrops of native stone as a nod to both the bears' native habitat and Rock Creek's dramatic geology.

Bottom:
NBW designed custom railings to maximize visibility into the animal enclosures. The steel vertical elements house narrow lights for evening visitors, and the spans between are made of stainless-steel woven mesh for safe, open viewing.

Opposite top:
Parallel terraced viewing areas offer a broad range of views across lushly planted habitats, accommodating large groups of visitors in an atmosphere that still feels intimate.

Opposite bottom:
Plan of the Asia Trail at the National Zoo

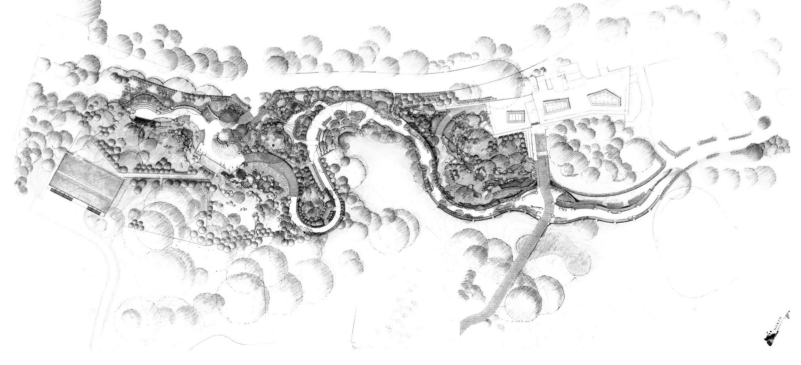

Top left:
Native beautyberry displays its fruit in front of fieldstone-filled gabion walls.

Top right:
A dried-bamboo structure designed by NBW shades interpretive panels.

Bottom left:
Towers of bamboo mark entrances to the exhibit. These bundles bound with copper bands demonstrate the amount of bamboo an adult giant panda can consume in one day.

Bottom right:
NBW designed a curb rail in steel and bamboo to be an attractive but efficient border to the public paths, deterring visitors from leaving the trail.

Opposite:
A high gabion wall links the upper and lower viewing terraces of the giant panda enclosure.

Top left:
The fishing cat habitat emulates key aspects of the creatures' natural environment and allows the animals to express their fundamental behaviors.

Top right:
The habitat design for the often shy red panda provides ample opportunity for these animals to be higher than adjacent visitors, increasing the bears' public visibility.

Bottom left:
The Asian otter exhibit successfully encourages play and basking, providing views of the animals' endearing behavior.

Bottom right:
Glass-walled viewing areas reveal the underwater world of the otters.

Opposite:
Massive steel ribs and cables form trellises designed to bolster abundant bamboo plantings along the trail and create an enclosing tunnel of green.

Top:
Horticultural pairings of Asiatic and mid-Atlantic trees, shrubs, and perennials are a lesson in disjunctive evolution (a theory that plants from different parts of the globe may have descended from a common parent species).

Bottom:
The planting design of the Asia Trail, which includes these late-blooming Japanese anemones, has impact throughout the four seasons, at large and small scales.

Opposite:
Thanks to nearly transparent fencing and rails as well as continuous plantings that bridge divisions between enclosures, the visitors' experience is marked more by inclusion than the sense of separation found in many zoos.

Right:
Large gabion walls made of steel, wire mesh, and fieldstone negotiate steep gradients and offer a textural contrast to more naturalistic plantings and stone outcrops.

Opposite:
The design of the Asia Trail celebrates the natural grade changes of the Rock Creek valley while emphasizing dramatic views of the park's topography and water features.

Overleaf:
Trellises create a memorable passageway into the habitats while providing structure for the bamboo in snow and heavy rains.

Flight 93 National Memorial

Location: Shanksville, Pennsylvania
Site area: 2,200 acres
Project dates: 2005–present

On a lonely field in western Pennsylvania are the beginnings of one of America's newest and most emotionally resonant national parks. The heart of the park is the exact location where forty people lost their lives on September 11, 2001, on United Airlines Flight 93. The goal of the park and its design is to commemorate and honor the heroes of that day and their struggle with their attackers.

Paul Murdoch Architects, one of five finalists in the first stage of a national competition in 2004, invited NBW to collaborate on their final competition entry. After winning the competition in the spring of 2005, the firms embarked as a team on the design and construction of this remarkable landscape memorial.

The Crash Site composes the memorial's center. A low, tilted wall and a moat structure planted with red-twig dogwood marks this territory and limits the visiting public's access to the site. Inscribed on a taller white marble site wall that traces the flight path are the names of each of the forty passengers and crew members who lost their lives. A ceremonial gate through the wall allows access for family members to the Crash Site, while a larger, publicly accessible area of the park surrounds this inner core. A great one-mile arc of trees will define a Field of Honor that served as witness to the catastrophic event. A double circular allée of red maples, reinforced by forty groves of forty trees, is planned to embrace the field and to give form to the disturbed site, which until the crash had been an extensive coal strip-mining operation in the process of restoration.

The first phase of the Flight 93 memorial has been completed. Adjacent to the white marble Memorial Wall is a black granite paved surface; a plaza offers seating near an entry portal with parking areas and adjacent raingardens. The plant palette for this first phase was derived from the species and plant communities that grow naturally in this area. New plantings will focus on the addition of wildflowers and warm-season grass meadows, newly created wetland margins, and tree and shrub plantings that include rows and bosques of planetrees, river birches, sumacs, and witchhazels. These trees reinforce the architectural alignment of entry paths and portals into the Memorial Plaza, augmented by more randomly spaced plantings of serviceberries, oaks, hackberries, elms, pines, beeches, and black gums that exist as remnants of the adjacent forested margins.

As subsequent phases of the project commence with the introduction of even bolder gestures, including a circular promenade of mature trees in a dramatic commemorative arrangement, a learning and visitor's center at the arrival point, and a Tower of Voices at the park's entrance, the memorial will flourish as a place of quiet visitation and contemplation for many years to come.

PRIMARY MATERIALS

Black granite pavement

Concrete walls

Concrete with an exposed-aggregate finish

Crushed-limestone walks and trails

Sandstone benches

PLANT LIST

Acer rubrum (red maple)

Acer saccharum (sugar maple)

Amelanchier spp. (serviceberry)

Cornus stolonifera (red osier dogwood)

Fagus grandifolia (American beech)

Hamamelis virginiana (American witchhazel)

Native warm-season meadow grasses and wildflowers

Nyssa sylvatica (black gum)

Platanus x *acerifolia* 'Columbia' ('Columbia' London planetree)

Rhus aromatica (fragrant sumac)

Top:
A lower parking area and entry pavilion are framed by a native meadow, planetrees, and three sweetgums in an NBW design that was originally presented for the World Trade Center memorial site.

Bottom:
The white marble Memorial Wall forms the western edge of the Memorial Plaza. Each panel displays the name of one of the forty passengers.

Top:
A rendering of Phase I of the memorial shows the Field of Honor, Memorial Plaza, Memorial Wall, and Crash Site.

Bottom:
Plan of the Flight 93 National Memorial

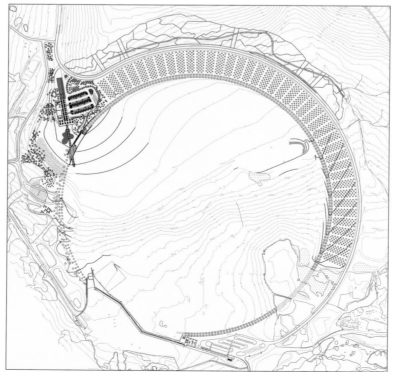

Right:
The Memorial Wall and plaza appear in repose at dusk, with the Crash Site to the left.

Opposite top:
Hemlocks form a backdrop to the Memorial Plaza and the Crash Site.

Opposite bottom:
President and Mrs. Obama visited the memorial on September 11, 2011, for the ceremony marking the tenth anniversary of the attacks.

Overleaf:
A rendering shows how the impressive ring of red maples mediates between the forty groves and the Field of Honor. The allée of trees with its bright red fall foliage links the visitor's center with the Crash Site along a one-mile walk.

Left:
Sandstone blocks, witchhazel, sumac, and planetrees frame the entry portal.

Opposite top and bottom:
A walkway tracing the edge of the Crash Site passes through the entry portal to the Memorial Plaza.

Top:
The expanse of the Field of Honor, planted
with wildflowers and native grasses, leads
the eye toward the Crash Site beyond.

Bottom:
Vivid coreopsis are part of the wildflower
and native-grass mix selected for the Field
of Honor.

Opposite top:
Visitors assemble along the Flight Path; a
ceremonial gate made of hemlock marks
an entrance into the Crash Site for family
members.

Opposite bottom:
The defining ridge that embraces the
memorial can be seen from the Field of
Honor.

Overleaf:
A large wildflower meadow within the
memorial's Field of Honor serves as a
foreground to the central Memorial Plaza.

Citygarden

Location: St. Louis, Missouri
Site area: 2.9 acres
Project dates: 2008–2010

Gateway Mall stretches from the Mississippi River and Eero Saarinen's famous arch to St. Louis's City Hall and historic Union Station. Before the execution of NBW's design, these fifteen city blocks were surprisingly underused and derelict, given their prime location in the center of a major city. In the mall's middle was a two-block, three-acre vacant space characterized by empty lawn and struggling street trees, with a perimeter bound by city streets and very tall corporate and civic office buildings. The Gateway Foundation, a private foundation with a large collection of outdoor sculpture and a considerable commitment to civic improvement, sponsored the effort to turn these blocks into a sculpture garden and public park. After a national search, the foundation selected NBW to be the landscape architects for the project.

A major challenge lay in placing two dozen large-scale sculptures in a city park that is purposefully neither fenced nor gated. The foundation wanted the space to feel open and inviting, requiring that it be fully accessible to the public. It also resisted installing the off-putting signage that typically discourages engagement with public art, for either the sculptures or the garden's fountains, basins, and scrims. The foundation's goal was to encourage citizens to spend time downtown, with the hope that increased activity would help to accelerate the ongoing revitalization of this part of the city.

Since St. Louis is famously hot in the summer, the designers knew that abundant shade and cooling water would be required to make the park a success. The landscape architects decided to exaggerate a slight grade change of about six feet from one corner of the property to the other by lifting the park's northeast corner, where a cafe sits, so that visitors can enjoy an expansive view. This raising of the grade also helps to distinguish the more urban, terraced northern side of Citygarden from the lower, more green and open portions to the south side.

At one time, the two central blocks of the site had supported a range of buildings, which were razed to make way for the original park. After researching 1916 Sanborn maps, the designers adapted the traces of those obliterated property boundaries and a system of no-longer-extant alleyways as guidelines for a pattern of paths and distinct planting beds that structured the central and south areas. Two stone walls that define the three precincts of the garden echo the nearby river systems that influenced the settlement of St. Louis. The great limestone bluffs found along reaches of the Mississippi and Missouri rivers inspired a massive arcing limestone wall that separates the two districts of Citygarden: the Upland, an urban area near the cafe, and the lower Flood Plain, which contains the largest sculptures and the majority of the garden's water elements. Defining the edge of the Flood Plain lawn is an eleven-hundred-foot-long seat wall made of greenish-black granite. The low wall meanders in oxbow curves reminiscent of the region's streams and remnant rivers. The River Terrace flower gardens, with species arranged in blocks, refer to the agricultural lands bordering the

PRIMARY MATERIALS

Bronze

Minnesota granite (Mesabi Black, Lake
    Superior)

Missouri limestone

Pennsylvania bluestone

Stainless steel

PLANTS

Acer rubrum 'Red Sunset' ('Red Sunset' red
    maple)

Amelanchier laevis (Allegheny serviceberry)

Asclepias tuberosa (butterfly milkweed)

Betula nigra 'Dura Heat' ('Dura Heat' river
    birch)

Buxus 'Green Gem' ('Green Gem' boxwood)

Cercis canadensis (Eastern redbud)

Cladrastis kentukea (Kentucky yellowwood)

Echinacea spp. (coneflower)

Eupatorium maculatum 'Gateway'
    (joe-pye weed)

Fothergilla gardenii (dwarf fothergilla)

Ginkgo biloba 'Autumn Gold'

Gleditsia triacanthos (honey locust)

Gymnocladus dioicus (Kentucky coffeetree)

Hamamelis virginiana (American witchhazel)

Heuchera spp. (coralbells)

Hydrangea quercifolia 'Sikes Dwarf' ('Sikes
    Dwarf' oakleaf hydrangea)

Itea virginica 'Henry's Garnet' ('Henry's
    Garnet' Virginia sweetspire)

Juncus effusus (soft rush)

Lobelia cardinalis (cardinal flower)

Monarda spp. (bee balm)

Panicum virgatum 'Shenandoah'
    ('Shenandoah' switchgrass)

Quercus bicolor (swamp white oak)

Quercus coccinea (scarlet oak)

Citygarden incorporates twenty-four masterworks of modern and contemporary art, including this LED piece by Julian Opie.

great river corridors. At the western end of the park, the designers sited a ten-foot mount planted with a grove of river birch and ferns, heucheras, and hellebores. This archetypal landform recalls the neighboring Cahokia Native American mound cities of ancient times. All the topographical innovations highlight and reinforce the placement of sculptures, some of which are meant to be viewed in isolation while others are sited to appear in relation to one another.

NBW worked closely with horticulturists at the renowned Missouri Botanical Garden to establish a planting strategy that would succeed in the harshness of this particular urban environment. They focused on native trees, shrubs, grasses, and wildflowers as much as possible so that visitors could appreciate a palette of regional wildflowers that are unexpected in a municipal setting. Cardinal flowers, juncus, panicum, bee balm, and joe-pye weed now dominate the plantings. The site was cursed with poor soil degraded by years of compaction and construction debris, so the design team proposed the addition of three to four feet of new, well-drained, fertile soil. Several soil types were used to compose the distinct planting zones throughout the site. These strategies, along with a program of green roofs and permeable pavements, help further the park's agenda of sustainability. But perhaps the most significant endeavor is the installation of 235 trees (swamp live oak, scarlet oak, red maple, sugar maple, river birch, yellowwood, hornbeam, redbud, sweetbay, Kentucky coffeetree, honey locust, ginkgo, and serviceberry) and 1,300 shrubs (clethra, fothergilla, itea, oakleaf hydrangea, and witchhazel). In addition, a host of primarily native perennials, groundcovers, and grasses thrive in the urban setting. Throughout, city-dwellers and tourists enjoy the abundant references to geology, hydrology, and local botany that lend this formerly orphaned plaza a sense of place and meaning.

Top:
A broad terrace and stair form an informal theater at the heart of Citygarden. The design of the masonry work throughout the landscape emphasizes regional stone and the sculptural qualities of walls, benches, and stairs.

Bottom:
A range of textures and finishes highlights the versatility of regional limestone; a massive LED screen displays a variety of video art.

Opposite top:
A cafe terrace provides outdoor seating shaded by honey locusts and presents a sweeping view out across Citygarden.

Opposite bottom:
Plan of Citygarden

Overleaf:
An overview of Citygarden reveals its intricate geometry, which is based both on local geologic features and the palimpsest of original property and building outlines that were revealed through NBW's extensive site research.

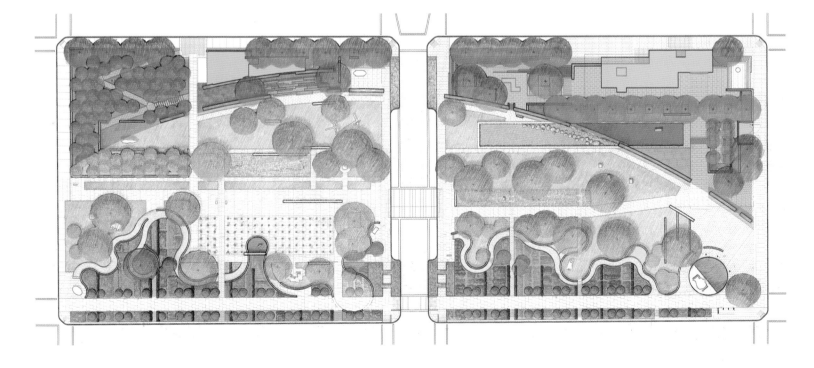

Top:
The massive limestone blocks that form the garden's arc wall recall the cliffs and bluffs along the Mississippi River, which were a factor in the location and development of St. Louis.

Bottom:
A view through the steel rings of a sculpture by Bernar Venet reveals a six-foot waterfall linking reflecting pools.

Opposite:
A central angled walkway follows the path of a former alleyway through the warehouses that once filled Citygarden's site.

Top:
Several sculptural works have become beloved destinations for children and are a reminder of the Gateway Foundation's commitment to promoting an unfettered connection between art and the public.

Bottom:
The planting design of Citygarden emphasizes the four-season variations of the region's native plant palette.

Opposite:
An allée of *Ginkgo biloba* lends structure to the exuberant perennial gardens and forms a graceful tree-lined walk toward Eero Saarinen's Gateway Arch.

Right:
The garden's mount is dominated by an equestrian sculpture by Mimmo Paladino. Its elevation offers striking views over the park.

Opposite top:
A low, curving wall forms intimate garden rooms and creates seating for individuals and small groups. Tall spires of loosely growing perennials such as Russian sage complement the sleek modernity of the stone.

Opposite bottom:
The highly polished, winding granite seat evokes the reflections of the Mississippi and its convoluted oxbow tributaries.

Overleaf:
Long axes of trees punctuated by gardens and shrubs establish an emphatic visual rhythm that leads down to the monumental archway and the river.

PART III:
COMMUNITY
Moist Surfaces, Watery Connections, Porous Borders

Elizabeth Meyer

Beyond our home landscapes of gardens and yards, where we gather with family and close friends, we live, work, and move within a vast and complex territory of public places. The landscapes between buildings—whether streets, alleys, parks, plazas, quadrangles, or courtyards—are social spaces where strangers encounter one another, individuals interact, and public identities are formed. This extended home—or community—takes place in varied geographies and ecologies that are a topographic bas relief upon which a landscape architect makes new marks. It is also a hydrological system within which a landscape architect alters the flow of water as well as people and cars. The landscape's found and constructed character, its structure and function, are more than a background for quotidian life. The designed landscape affects the range and quantity of interactions and the type of affiliations through which community is built and experienced.

NBW has expanded and enriched a community through their designs in projects including WaterColor, the Dell at the University of Virginia (UVA), and the Campbell Hall landscape at UVA. Through the designs of a suburb, a park, and a school, they have created communities that are more than collections of people who share a social or institutional mission. These communities are based on relationships among people, bodies of water, and their watersheds. At a basic level, the projects move away from the standard practice of hardening and drying surfaces between buildings. In the ecological models that dominated our recent past, this rainfall would have been channeled into drains and gutters and moved quickly through a system of below-ground stormwater pipes, causing erosion and flooding downstream. Instead, rainfall is allowed to gather in small, moist, concave raingardens or larger ponds that detain water. These on-site water bodies collect rainfall that percolates into the ground (supporting plant growth and increasing biodiversity) and gather wildlife and social life around their edges.

NBW is not alone in adopting these practices; performative green infrastructure systems are ubiquitous in contemporary landscape architecture. But few firms have been as successful in considering the civic and social aspects of integrating best practices for stormwater management into their work. Even fewer firms have been as critical and creative in imagining constructed waterworks in relationship to adjacent or surrounding established cultural landscapes characterized by nonsustaining site planning and landscape design.

The success of WaterColor and the two University of Virginia projects owes much to their connections to—and differences from—two well-known and loved communities: Seaside, Florida (designed by Duany Plater-Zyberk [DPZ] in the

Top:
The design elements of the Dell at the University of Virginia emerge directly from its water-quality mechanisms, including those for aeration, desedimentation, and stormwater retention, as well as from an early twentieth-century garden ruin found on the site.

Bottom:
Rather than clearing native scrub-oak and pine woodlands, NBW incorporated the many existing groves of trees into the parks, walks, and trails of its master plan for WaterColor in Santa Rosa Beach, Florida.

1980s), and the Academical Village at UVA (designed by Thomas Jefferson in the 1820s). The typological mixes of landscape that compose both this renowned suburb and this historic campus depend on terracing the ground to reduce wetness and precisely manipulating each site's microtopography to drain rainfall and increase dryness at all costs. In other words, the innovations at Seaside and UVA are ecological-system alterations as well as cultural-landscape transformations. NBW did more than insert new ecological and hydrological processes into their community designs. They created new landscape details, typologies, and experiences that reimagine familiar cultural landscape forms and practices by blending them with contemporary innovations in revealing ecological processes.

WaterColor, a second-home community, is located in the Florida Panhandle and adjacent to Seaside, which is one of the earliest examples of American New Urbanism. Since its design in the early 1980s, Seaside has been the model for hundreds of new communities across the nation. Characterized by walkable blocks (instead of automobile-centric cul-de-sacs) and conventional landscape types such as tree-lined streets with sidewalks, residential alleys, and public gardens and parks, New Urbanist communities dramatically altered debates about the form and character of American residential living.

Most of these debates have focused on the architectural style of DPZ's houses, but when I first saw their projects in a Harvard Graduate School of Design exhibition in the early 1990s, I was appalled by their landscape strategies. Each community was characterized by geometric patterns of lots, streets, blocks, and bounded parks. Its center was structured around the clear, geometric figure of a square or semicircular public building or space. And its edges were determined by what DPZ described as the "awkward" and "irregular" conditions of its site. What DPZ saw as awkward (because a repetitive field pattern of streets and blocks could not continue), most landscape architects would see as topographic variations of high and low, dry and wet, woods and wetland, which could be integrated into unique and site-specific building and landscape configurations.

WaterColor, designed twenty years after Seaside by NBW in collaboration with Jaque Robertson (a founding partner of Cooper, Robertson & Partners and former dean of the UVA School of Architecture), is a remarkable community, worthy of its 2003 American Society of Landscape Architects design award. The design is exemplary for its infusion of hydrological innovation into the New Urbanist form language; in doing so it creates new experiences of landscape and of community. Public spaces and walking paths in WaterColor are more prevalent, and private lots smaller, than in Seaside. The walking and cycling network through WaterColor is interwoven with a network of small and large, constructed and found wetlands—stepped water channels, geometrically shaped water basins, and a lake. These watery surfaces and porous edges, which perform the ecological functions of collection, aeration, filtration, and cleansing, are also important social spaces that choreograph movement and encounters among residents and guests. WaterColor is a place that not only benefits from its waterfront location but also contributes to it.

The Dell and the UVA School of Architecture's Campbell Hall play a similar role on the UVA Grounds—one that carries much historical weight. The UVA Academical Village is one of eight cultural landscapes located in the United States that are designated as UNESCO World Heritage sites. The core of the Grounds is a twenty-acre complex of buildings and landscapes interwoven at a scale not common in most university campuses. Intimate alleys and courtyards, gardens bounded by serpentine walls, colonnades and arcades, an irregularly spaced allée, and a tall grove of trees weave in and around ten small pavilions, residential colonnades, and arcades. This fabric of built elements and landscape connects the central rotunda and terraced lawn to its topographic and urban context. But water is invisible on this constructed Piedmont ridge. It moves quickly from roof to gutter to ground, from surface to subsurface, with little tectonic expression.

The Dell and the Campbell Hall demonstration gardens are two of the first designed landscapes on the UVA Grounds to slow the movement of water off site, to reveal the rain-to-roof-to-groundwater cycle, and to incorporate it into the public-space network of the Grounds. Campbell Hall has housed the school of architecture since the early 1970s. Like many buildings of its period, it concealed the relationship between the rain that falls on its large flat roof and the stormwater it pipes in to the city storm-sewer system. In the early 2000s, the school commissioned a collaborative team of three architects and a landscape architect to plan and design two additions to this large, concrete-frame structure, as well as a series of intermediate public spaces between the additions and the surrounding hillside. NBW's outdoor rooms—a tree-lined walk, a south-facing terrace, a sunken work court, an outdoor classroom, a raingarden, and a shady courtyard—expand the social life of the school from the studios and hallways out into the campus. Outdoor activity moves around the building, depending on the season and schedule of classes. As students and faculty appropriate the adjacent series of outdoor rooms for work, study, and play, they are exposed to a set of details unlike any others around the Grounds. Channels in the street curb and gutter enter the outdoor rooms through narrow rills, which sustain raingardens of native grasses and forbs, and through weeps in stone retaining walls stained with watermarks of prior downpours. Close to the south face of the faculty office addition, water collects and percolates through the ground, recharging it. The south entrance to the second floor passes between one-hundred-foot-long dry gabion walls that line the service drive and a terraced, linear raingarden before crossing a short, wooden bridge that spans the moist ground below. The flow of water, students, and faculty occurs within one spatial volume; stormwater is not merely an infrastructural concern or a nuisance to be diverted out of sight of the university's public spaces. Water, from rainfall to surfacewater to groundwater, is both a landscape material and a shaper of experience that expands the architecture-school community beyond the social and intellectual to include the hydrological and bioregional.

The Dell is located to the west of and downhill from Campbell Hall and the Academical Village in a stream valley that connects the central Grounds to an urban forest—Observatory Hill, on the western boundary of the university. The Dell project remade a degraded stream valley (with much of the stream suppressed in below-ground pipes) into a park that now forms a porous border separating the neighborhood, the campus, and the urban forest. While the idea of a stormwater park in this location was part of earlier planning studies conducted by Andropogon, Judith Nitsch, and Cahill Associates for Mary Hughes in the university architect's office, it was NBW and their consultants Biohabitats who gave formal expression to this new landscape typology and experience. From the juxtaposition of earthen terraces—akin to those on the Academical Village's lawn, and part of the Virginia cultural landscape since the seventeenth century, with sloping banks that form the complex geometry of the Dell pond—to the stonework of the pond's overlook and rill, the Dell is replete with memories and traces of the surrounding cultural landscape, new and familiar at the same time.

I can speak to the ways it has altered the sense of community, as I live along the Dell's western edge. Nursery-school children, elderly neighbors, environmental-science students, football-game tailgaters, birdwatchers, sunbathers, young anglers, herons, ducks, and muskrats gather around and throughout the Dell. Ten years ago, it was a grassy valley floor that functioned as the demilitarized zone between the neighborhood and the Grounds. Today, it serves as more of a threshold, as well as a prominent reminder of the network of urban streams that lies hidden in the wooded valleys behind so many neighborhoods in

Charlottesville, 70 percent of which are considered degraded and polluted by the State of Virginia's criteria. The rise of the pond's water level after rainfall and its drop during droughts registers these natural phenomena in ways that are palpable and playful. After a particularly violent storm last spring, I found myself walking to the Dell to observe the stream pouring through the rill's scupper and over the weir between the settling basin and the lower pond. I was surrounded by people from neighborhoods near and far; a former student was there with his children, who were captivated by this evidence of the storm's delayed power, close enough to touch. This porous border, this watery surface was binding them to their home, their watershed, at the same time it was binding us to one another. Yes, our community landscapes are places we explore as children, finding freedoms close to home. But they are also places where we develop roots and connections to other people and to the territory, the watershed, and the region that is our home, as much as our own houses are.

Overleaf:
Children explore the spillway between the settlement basin and the stormwater-retention area of The Dell.

Campbell Hall at the University of Virginia

Location: Charlottesville, Virginia
Site area: 1/2 acre
Project dates: 2003–2008

In this long-evolving project, NBW collaborated with several members of the University of Virginia's architecture faculty to design a series of outdoor spaces surrounding the School of Architecture. The project's overarching mission was to highlight the positive relationship between the fields of architecture and landscape architecture at the university.

The school was in need of more space for faculty offices, as well as review and seminar rooms. The firm's charge was to extend the engagement of students and faculty outside of university buildings and to design outdoor classrooms, work terraces, and gathering places. Students had engaged with the existing landscape—a difficult, steep, and narrow site—only occasionally, due to its significant change in grade (a forty-foot drop in elevation across its entire span). The site's usefulness was compromised by this inaccessible terrain with its unarticulated, unshaded pockets of land.

The landscape architects created four distinct and usable outdoor levels, each corresponding to one of the four floors of the architecture school. NBW looked outside the site boundaries to the greater university context for design cues. They delineated the precincts by means of an allée of sugar maples lining a walk at the highest ground, a work terrace of simple gravel with a grove of hornbeams that provide shade at an intermediate level, and a dramatically compressed outdoor classroom that expresses the geology of locally quarries at the school's second-floor level. This room includes a slate wall and chalk for drawing lessons and a group of monolithic soapstone boulders and ledges that project from the floor and walls of the room.

A terraced bioretention garden completes the landscape composition at the western edge of the site. It treats stormwater as it flows down the incline through a series of low concrete weir walls that demarcate several planted basins. Gabion walls (whose permeability maximizes the flow of water into the bioretention planting beds) form a boundary between the native species and the roadside. Water is collected from the school's roof and parking lots and then sluiced to a gravel rill; the water is then directed into raingardens, which are planted with a mosaic of little bluestem grass, sensitive fern, cardinal flower, itea, and blue-eyed grass under a canopy of red maple and river birch. The area makes a dramatic transition over the course of the year, as spring perennials and grasses gradually obscure the concrete weirs that are so evident as structuring elements in the winter months.

On the east side of the building, a limited palette of primitive (early-evolution) plants such as ginkgo trees, ferns, and horsetail grass are used as expressive linear elements within a precisely defined and constricted architectural setting. On the higher west side, sumac, blueberries, switchgrass, amsonia, iris, redbuds, serviceberries, basswood, and sugar maples deliver a mixed mesophytic lushness during the summer months and a brilliant show in the autumn. The different planting areas serve

PRIMARY MATERIALS

Bluestone pavement

Concrete paving with diagonal crushed-stone joints or saw-cut score lines

Concrete stepped ramp with stone riser

Concrete weir walls

Crushed honeystone walk

Gabion walls filled with native stone

Metal guardrails and handrails

Soapstone walls, ledges, and boulders

PLANTS

Acer rubrum (red maple)

Acer saccharum (sugar maple)

Amelanchier laevis (Allegheny serviceberry)

Andropogon virginicus (broomsedge bluestem)

Carpinus caroliniana (American hornbeam)

Equisetum spp. (horsetail)

Ginkgo biloba 'Princeton Sentry'

Itea virginica (Virginia sweetspire)

Lobelia cardinalis (cardinal flower)

Onoclea sensibilis (sensitive fern)

Rhus aromatica (fragrant sumac)

Rhus glabra (smooth sumac)

Schizachyrium scoparium (little bluestem)

Tilia americana (American basswood)

Vaccinium spp. (blueberry)

Steel-wire gabions filled with regional fieldstone mark the boundary between a bioretention garden and the street, allowing stormwater to move laterally into treatment gardens.

as a demonstration garden for students as they work outdoors or take part in open-air classroom sessions. Even though it covers only half an acre, the project makes a positive contribution to slowing down erosion and treating runoff as it passes through the site. The hope is that this modest transformation of the Chesapeake Bay's upper watershed will encourage additional downstream adaptations of overengineered campus and community environments and ultimately improve the water quality of the compromised stream and river systems that support the entire watershed. The Campbell Hall landscapes are intended to promote the spirit of ecological remediation through powerful design.

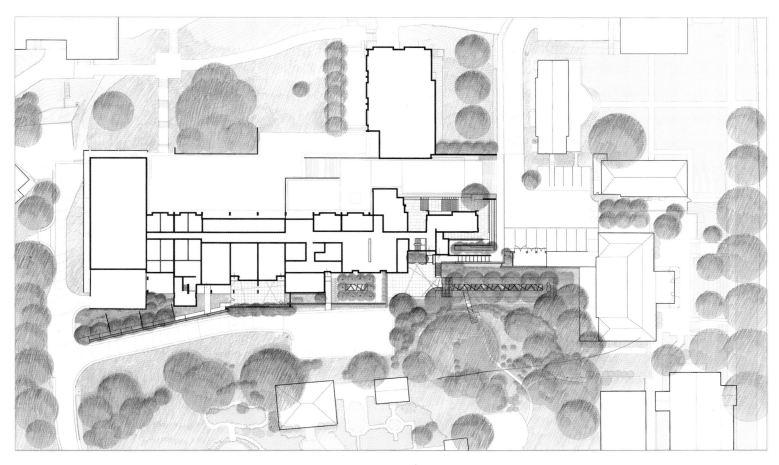

Above:
Plan of the Campbell Hall landscapes

Opposite:
An outdoor classroom is the site of multiple sustainable initiatives. Glass panels pivot across the Campbell Hall facade to allow natural airflow and shading, slate cladding heats domestic hot water, and the course of stormwater is made visible through a gravel channel and a retaining wall with scuppers.

Right:
Locally quarried soapstone blocks are carefully arranged to create an abstracted geologic section. An aperture in the boulders acts as a scupper during storms, allowing rainwater collected on the terraces above to flow into a gravel channel and on to a bioswale for treatment.

Opposite top:
Soapstone boulders are positioned as if to emerge directly from the terrace pavement. Stones were chosen to display both natural faces and marks of the quarrying process.

Opposite bottom:
Concrete retaining walls support a shelf that allows students to display design boards, models, or impromptu still-lifes.

Right:
Concrete walls structure and separate infiltration pools. Small weirs allow water to pass through the system during severe storms, preventing damage to the pools.

Opposite top:
Four bioretention basins are planted with hydric-adapted native species including cardinal flower, little bluestem, sensitive fern, Virginia sweetspire, and red maple. These terraces provide seasonal interest, improved water quality, and stormwater infiltration.

Opposite bottom:
Native plants such as *Itea virginica* and *Schizachyrium scoparium* tolerate standing water during periods of infiltration and also thrive during drier times.

Top:
Concrete walls, ramps, and plantings structure a simple amphitheater and establish a court that frames the Campbell Hall addition.

Bottom:
The striking form of horsetail grass fills a bed between ramps, providing texture for the shady area.

Opposite:
Rows of ginkgoes form a green wall above ramps underplanted with horsetail grass. These ancient plants, which have not significantly evolved in millions of years, convey a narrative of continuity.

Top:
The allée above Campbell Hall provides a
shady gathering area for students.

Bottom:
A dense planting of horsetail grass and
ferns will grow into an informal hedge that
acts as a green barrier.

Opposite:
The pavement of the allée above Campbell
Hall is laced with small strips of permeable
crushed stone. Their placement was
determined by the many utility lines buried
beneath the site.

Overleaf:
A work terrace adjacent to design studios
offers a shady environment for model
building, construction, and painting.
Outdoor lighting accommodates the
students' late work hours.

The Dell at the University of Virginia

Location: Charlottesville, Virginia
Site area: 11 acres
Project dates: 2003–2007

At the University of Virginia, a narrow stream valley runs from the forested Observatory Hill past parking lots, roads, and dormitories through a site with a very long and rather checkered past. The formerly sylvan site's history of very pragmatic use dates back to Thomas Jefferson's day, when a now-buried pond served as a water source and ice-skating venue. In the early twentieth century, a university professor built a house adjacent to the site and developed an Italianate garden with walls, pavilions, and garden follies. After 1929, when a new road was constructed nearby, the garden fell into muddy disuse as the landscape began to deteriorate into a collection of invasive plants and ruined structures. Over the years, most of the stream was piped and sent underground according to standard engineering practices of the day. Ponds were drained, the valley was filled, and terraces for dormitories and fields for intramural athletics were created.

NBW was engaged to transform the neglected and underused site—which is near one of the primary entrances to the campus—into a major attraction for students, faculty, and nearby residents. The firm, working from a visionary university-sponsored stormwater master plan and collaborating with several innovative hydrology and civil-engineering consultants, designed a park that daylighted twelve-hundred feet of the piped stream—ensuring sustainability and restoring the site's former beauty.

A second goal was to highlight the far-reaching interconnectedness of the waters in the region. The designers created a stormwater system that collects and conveys water from an eighty-acre watershed of Piedmont forest, suburban homes, yards, campus parking lots, roads, and building rooftops. This hydrology is redirected through the reclaimed stream with its adjacent raingardens and then dramatically funneled through a stone channel that cascades the water into a sediment forebay located just above the three-quarter-acre pond, which is positioned at the lowest part of the site. From this catchment area with its series of check dams and weirs, the improved water heads to Meadow Creek, which in turn flows to the Rivanna and James Rivers and the distant Chesapeake Bay.

The stormwater pond takes cues from previous water-retention impoundments that had been in place in Jefferson's day, but the form of the basin deliberately expresses a contemporary interpretation of adjacent conditions. The southern and eastern edges of the pond are defined by taut, linear lawn terraces that reflect the university's geometry and orientation, while the sinuous and exuberantly planted northern edge is articulated to represent the meandering natural order of stream alignments and Piedmont topography. Shenandoah fieldstone walls reference local styles of wallmaking that can be found in a nearby Civil War cemetery. The firm has created a hybrid eco-botanic garden—a cross between a park and a working remedial landscape—to responsibly process institutional runoff.

PRIMARY MATERIALS

Bluestone weir caps and pond edges

Concrete channels, retaining walls, and walks

Fieldstone walls

Metal water scuppers

Treated-wood bridges

PLANTS

Amelanchier spp. (serviceberry)

Betula nigra 'Heritage' ('Heritage' river birch)

Cornus spp. (dogwood)

Eupatorium spp. (joe-pye weed)

Ilex glabra (inkberry)

Ilex verticillata (American winterberry)

Itea virginica (Virginia sweetspire)

Liriodendron tulipifera (tulip tree)

Magnolia spp. (sweetbay and southern magnolia)

Myrica cerifera (southern wax myrtle)

Panicum spp. (switchgrass)

Platanus occidentalis (American planetree)

Pontederia cordata (pickerel weed)

Rhus aromatica (fragrant sumac)

Salix spp. (willow)

Taxodium spp. (bald and pond cypress)

Viburnum spp.

This aerial view highlights the designed juxtaposition between the meandering north side of the Dell, reflective of typical stream morphology, and the linear south side that responds to the historic grid of the university.

As part of the collective memory of the site and its history, several elements of the original owner's garden were retained and featured, while others proved too difficult or expensive to restore. The vocabulary of plants emphasizes Virginia natives, often highlighting related species from the same genus—such as magnolia and amelanchier—that derive from three distinct physiographic zones: the upland Blue Ridge mountains, the intermediate Piedmont, and the coastal plain. The beautifully planted pond now draws abundant wildlife such as red foxes, blue herons, ducks, turtles, and fish and has become popular with neighborhood and university residents as a destination for strolling. The new Dell is proving to be a valuable teaching space for faculty and students and—perhaps even more notably—an invaluable hub for the various communities of people, plants, and animals that populate this reinvigorated environment.

Top:
A four-foot-high spillway aerates and oxygenates streamwater as it falls into a sediment basin; from there, the flow drops quietly into a retention pond.

Bottom:
 A small pedestrian bridge links two contrasting waterways—the meandering creek and the constructed channel above the waterfall.

Opposite top:
The reconstructed creek makes its way through native plantings of river birch, winterberry, and meadow grasses at the edge of a small soccer field, providing a much-needed winter habitat for wildlife.

Opposite bottom:
Plan of The Dell

Top:
A winding path along one side of the retention basin provides ever-changing views, a seasonally diverse experience for visitors, and an important wildlife habitat, in contrast to the grassy slopes of the opposite shore, where students gather to enjoy the sun.

Bottom:
Distinct layers of native grasses contrast with the fall colors of *Itea virginica* and the semi-evergreen *Myrica cerifera* in the distance.

Opposite:
Spillways assist water filtration by aerating streamwater and removing sediment.

Overleaf:
NBW's visibly constructed landscape offers important ecological benefits without attempting to mimic nature entirely: pickerel weed, lizard tail, and native iris create a rich habitat for invertebrates and amphibians along the shore of the retention basin.

Top:
In winter the design of The Dell is brought
into relief as snowfall emphasizes the
contrast between curvilinear and straight
edges.

Bottom:
The retention basin features plants native
to Virginia's Tidewater region. Further
upstream the plant choices are drawn from
the state's Piedmont and Mountain regions.

Opposite:
Regionally gathered fieldstone forms an
elegant water channel.

Left:
A lush pondside planting showcases layers of flowering aquatic plants.

Opposite top:
Planted margins around the basin maximize habitats for invertebrates and amphibians rarely found on university campuses.

Opposite bottom:
Great Herons began enjoying their new habitat soon after construction was completed.

Overleaf:
A terraced slope steps down to the stone-lined water's edge, where an allée of water oaks recalls the alignment of Jefferson's grid structure at the nearby core of the University of Virginia.

WaterColor

Location: Santa Rosa Beach, Florida
Site area: 499 acres
Project dates: 1999–2008

In transforming a relatively flat, forested stretch of the Florida Panhandle on the Gulf Coast into a resort, retirement, and second-home community, NBW was conscientious about treading lightly on the land. Where some might have been tempted to design the usual ersatz paradise of imported palm trees and tropicals, the firm selected a palette of primarily native trees and shrubs to populate an expansive master plan of public gardens, town squares, parks, recreational pathways, and wetland areas. In the process, they established a new model for development in that part of Florida, recognizing local ecosystems as models to be celebrated and reinforced instead of as disposable commodities waiting to be swapped out for something more exotic.

Each system—from stormwater to wildlife and human activity to marine conditions—was examined holistically to involve minimal disruption to the site, which was then unpopulated but not pristine. Indeed, it had been a working pine-timber plantation owned by the St. Joe Company, one of Florida's largest landowners. The challenge for the primary architects and landscape architects was to create a desirable place for homeowners and visitors—replete with all the expected modern amenities—while also preserving the rural character and protecting natural resources and wildlife.

The site contained a range of growing conditions. In higher sandy or dry spots, yaupon holly, sand pine, and sand live oaks with their sinuous trunks exist near strikingly expressive stands of bald cypress, slash pine, and sweet bay magnolias that surround wetlands and a natural 220-acre lake. Stormwater and runoff are treated in distinctive raingardens and holding ponds that double as picturesque destinations for a large network of walking, jogging, and biking trails. A cohesive palette of species links the street plantings and public spaces, which are arranged in diverse configurations of circles, arcs, squares, and rectangles. These native plants might clipped to form low hedges or elsewhere encouraged to grow more naturalistically. The firm espouses a belief in using common plants in uncommon ways and vice versa.

The firm's collaboration with project architects Cooper, Robertson and Partners yielded a wide variety of design solutions. Groupings of closely spaced houses with screened porches surround different types of common areas that function as town greens for the residents, recreating the feeling of traditional Southern neighborhoods. It is a bold move to send people off their own properties instead of protecting them within the large, fenced private yards that so often inhibit community participation and social interaction in America. Instead of lawns, the shrubs, native groundcovers, and pine needles that are found in the surrounding forest understory blanket the ground. Many of the sidewalks are deliberately narrow and made of permeable crushed shells or sand. Parking lots are kept to a minimum to encourage walking; the design impetus is getting residents outside, out of their cars, and exploring the benefits of the location's weather and natural beauty.

PRIMARY MATERIALS

Ceramic tile fountain channels

Custom-color concrete pavers for vehicular drives and courts

Granite fountains

Painted wood fences

Sand and crushed-shell paths

Treated-pine boardwalks and bridges

PLANTS

Clethra alnifolia (summersweet)

Ilex verticillata (American winterberry)

Ilex vomitoria (Yaupon holly)

Magnolia grandiflora (Southern magnolia)

Muhlenbergia capillaris (hairawn muhly)

Myrica cerifera (Southern wax myrtle)

Pinus clausa (sand pine)

Pinus elliottii (slash pine)

Pinus palustris (longleaf pine)

Quercus virginiana (sand live oak)

Salvia spp. (ornamental sage)

Serenoa repens (saw palmetto)

Spartina spp. (cordgrass)

Taxodium distichum (bald cypress)

Gracefully curving boardwalks meander among existing trees and shrub masses, permitting visual access to fragile habitats without damaging them.

Top:
Wetland areas of the site were preserved and made accessible to visitors by raised walkways that pass over the existing native vegetation.

Bottom:
Large stands of native grasses and palmetto in the borders of the more public areas are constant reminders of the region's native plant community.

Opposite top:
Stands of slash pine and sand live oak were saved during construction and provide shade, scale, and a native context to the newly built Cerulean Park.

Opposite bottom:
Plan of WaterColor

Top:
A wooden decked bridge crosses an elliptical pool at the entrance to Cerulean Park, establishing a vocabulary of waterways, boardwalks, and regional plant species that are used throughout the development.

Bottom:
A simple carved-stone source fountain is reminiscent of both natural springs and the long tradition of Mediterranean and Islamic gardens.

Opposite:
Existing stands of sand live oak flank a three-hundred-foot-long canal lined with flowering plants that provide year-round color and texture in the warm climate.

Overleaf:
The sweeping spaces of Cerulean Park offer large areas for public gatherings, punctuated by the impressive silhouettes of mature trees.

Top and bottom:
Networks of boardwalks lace through broad
plantings of native grasses and marginal
wetland plants, which mitigate stormwater
flow while filtering groundwater and
providing important wildlife habitats.

Opposite:
Visitors to WaterColor discover a carefully
layered landscape with distinct areas of
forested wetland canopy, understory, and
grasses.

Top:
Water features such as this large freshwater
pond abound in a site located just steps
from the Gulf of Mexico.

Bottom:
Parallel bands of clipped bayberry hedges
and slash pines underplanted with palmetto
border a neighborhood park, providing
filtered views of the commons from
surrounding private houses.

Opposite:
The gnarled mature sand live oaks provide
a regional character to the neighborhoods
surrounding the parks.

Overleaf:
A rich vocabulary of landscape elements
enriches the entire project, as seen in
this garden area designed as a dragonfly
habitat. These include streets made of
concrete pavers, bands of stormwater
conveyances and infiltration swales,
groupings of trees, boardwalks, and natural
reserves for wild plants and animals.

PART IV:
FARM
Multifunctional Beauties

Elizabeth Meyer

When was the last time "Farm" was a chapter in a book on designed landscapes? It has been many decades since Garrett Eckbo, Daniel Kiley, and James Rose titled one of their cowritten articles "Landscape Design in the Rural Environment."[1] Or, shifting our gaze back toward the nineteenth century, we might recall the influence of agrarian matters on landscape architecture through the examples of A. J. Downing's writings about horticulture and pomology or Frederick Law Olmsted Sr.'s experiences in scientific farming. But a very old treatise, Thomas Whately's *Observations on Modern Gardening* (1770), best illuminates the aspirations of NBW's conservation agriculture studio and the projects included in this chapter. For Whately's treatise, a summary of the innovations found in eighteenth-century English landscape gardens, is organized around a series of chapters that address the essential media of the designed landscape—ground, water, trees, and rocks, as well as key areas for landscape design innovations—farm, garden, riding grounds, and park. The book concludes with an incredible chapter entitled "On Seasons," one of the first instances of a landscape-design treatise that speaks to the temporal, experiential, and affective aspects of the landscape medium.

What are we to make of an affiliation with the farm in the twenty-first century? NBW's conservation agriculture studio works with clients who own productive lands and working landscapes beyond homes and gardens, which have been the traditional focus of a landscape architect's rural commissions. These extended territories of fields, pastures, hedgerows, walled family cemeteries, orchards, woodlots, earthen-dam ponds, and meandering streams are the quintessential "second nature" described by Cicero and Jacopo Bonfadio and explicated by John Dixon Hunt in his brilliant essay "The Idea of a Garden and the Three Natures."[2] The form and processes of this type of landscape have been shaped by cultivation, grazing, and harvesting in response to human need, changing food preferences, and technological innovations. Neither the wild ("first nature") or the garden ("third nature"), the "second nature" of the rural landscape—and in particular, the farm—has its own beauty that emerges out of the intersection of practicality, need, and function with the slope and form of the terrain.

The rural cultural landscape has been an enduring source of inspiration for landscape architects across the world, from Daniel Kiley to Michel Corajoud to Kongjian Yu. For centuries, landscape architects have referenced the agricultural landscape and mined its planted form types and geometric patterns for design tactics and tropes. But few landscape architects have consciously taken on the shaping, transformation, and reformation of actual rural agricultural landscapes, in

Top:
An extensive network of shelter belts at Orongo Station in New Zealand protects citrus blossoms from damaging frosts and coastal winds.

Bottom:
Permanent sediment ponds formed by check dams constitute an important amphibious habitat along a stream formerly degraded by erosion.

1
Garrett Eckbo, Daniel Kiley, and James Rose, "Landscape Design in the Rural Environment," *Architectural Record*, August 1939, 68–74.

2
John Dixon Hunt, "The Idea of a Garden and the Three Natures," in *Greater Perfections: The Practice of Garden Theory* (Philadelphia: University of Pennsylvania Press, 2000), 32–75.

the manner currently practiced by NBW. Their vision for a collaborative practice involving landowners, conservation biologists, landscape ecologists, soil scientists, and farm managers has the potential to create regional landscape mosaics of more productive crops and herds, regenerative ecosystems, and healthier watersheds. As my visit to Orongo Station in New Zealand proved, it is also producing "slow landscapes," new forms and practices of sustainable, functional beauty that have their own pleasures.

If NBW's focus on the garden is not surprising, given Warren Byrd's academic background in horticulture and his teaching career within a school of architecture where thresholds between inside and outside and collaborations between architecture and landscape architecture have been central for decades, their fascination with the farm as a site of design inquiry and engagement is equally entangled with matters biographical as well as ideological. The addition of this new area of expertise, the conservation agriculture studio, is impossible to separate from NBW's office location in Charlottesville, a small city located in the Virginia Piedmont. This region is characterized by rolling pastures edged with Virginia red-cedar hedgerows, fallow fields washed with honey- to burnt-orange-colored sedge, and oak-hickory forest patches bounded on the west by the Blue Ridge Mountains. And if Byrd's and Woltz's combined sixty years of experience living and working in Charlottesville were not enough, Woltz's childhood experiences on a family-owned farm in North Carolina add depth to their innovative conservation agriculture studio. Woltz knows the rural landscape as a working landscape, as more than scenic vistas to be appreciated from the highways and byways of central Virginia when driving between Charlottesville and Washington, DC.

This focus of NBW's practice demonstrates the expanded contribution that landscape architects can make to the protection of rural cultural landscapes. The conservation agriculture studio creates frameworks for reconciling farming practices that privilege production of crops with conservation practices that protect wildlife habitat, ecosystems, and watersheds. These concerns are often at odds with one another. In projects such as Orongo Station and Seven Ponds Farm in Virginia, NBW is experimenting with principles and practices for the management of rural landscapes as interconnected spatial and functional matrices with flows of energy, nutrients, and species across boundaries of field, pasture, woodlot, forest, and riparian corridor. The agrarian landscape is appreciated for its multiple and simultaneous functions; it is a mixed-use landscape, not a series of separate uses within a landscape.

This spatial and functional lens for working within the rural agrarian landscape on the edges of our metropolitan areas is reminiscent of Charles Eliot's account of landscape architecture's role within the arts. In a talk to a group of architects, this young partner of Frederick Law Olmsted differentiated landscape architecture from garden design when he spoke of the landscape architect's ability to spatially and functionally organize the larger territory, declaring:

> whoever designs the arrangement of the buildings, ways, and green things of a farmstead, a country-seat, a village, a college, a world's fair or any other scene of human activity in such a way that beauty in the end shall spring forth from the happy marriage of the natural and the needful, is a successful landscape architect.[3]

Eliot reminds us that the beautiful is a not an a priori condition. It can be found in the expression of the necessary or functional. As needs change, conceptions and apprehensions of beauty also develop. As the landscape mosaic of gardens, fields, paddocks, pastures, woodlots, and forests is designed and managed in new ways to provide habitats for migrating birds, conditions for new crops, or hedgerow corridors for increased wildlife connectivity across a regional landscape, new large-scale landscapes are maturing that will evoke a sense of place that is different from that of the rural cultural landscapes of the past, but equally resonant. New concerns for plant and animal biodiversity and watershed quality are creating new aesthetic landscapes that express a community's health and function, as well as its productivity.

The multifunctional agrarian landscapes planned and designed by NBW with their clients are experimental grounds for a new kind of sustaining beauty. Their conservation agriculture studio claims a new role for landscape architects that was foreshadowed by modern landscape forebearers such as Whately and Eliot. Over the next few decades, the aggregate impact of the conservation agriculture studio has the potential to change landscape ecology and tactics of landscape design at a truly regional scale, and in doing so, to shape the experience of our metropolitan-rural periphery in slow but unexpectedly pleasurable ways.[4]

Overleaf:
A citrus orchard at Orongo Station was laid out by NBW to allow room for the native reforestation of the banks of the Maraetaha River. The design draws its elliptical shape from the natural curvature of the river.

3
Charles Eliot, "Landscape Architecture in Relation to Architecture," paper before the Boston Society of Architects, October 2, 1891, in Charles W. Eliot, *Charles Eliot, Landscape Architect* (Cambridge, MA: Harvard University Press, 1924), 363–367.

4
Elizabeth K. Meyer, "Slow Landscapes: A New Erotics of Sustainability," *Harvard Design Magazine* 31 (Fall/Winter 2009–2010): 22–31. This article focuses entirely on the Nick's Head property at Orongo Station.

Seven Ponds

Location: Albemarle County, Virginia
Site area: 133 acres
Project dates: 1997–present

NBW's work on this 150-acre farm in the Piedmont region of Virginia has evolved into an ongoing fifteen-year conversation between the landscape architects and their highly involved client about the cultivation of biodiversity. The project began as a fairly typical assignment to rework the gardens around a 1930s house. However, over time, the project has expanded to include all aspects of this large property, integrating them into a deeply rooted system of shared goals and a forward-looking environmental agenda.

The project's goals are simple and straightforward, but not easily accomplished. The first initiative aimed to reduce the amount of Japanese fescue grass, to convert grazing pastures to meadows of warm-season grasses and wildflowers, to reforest large swathes of woodland, and to manage the removal of invasive plant species. To track these efforts, the firm began a decade-long program with a local field biologist to study and count the plant species in ten-foot squares of meadow set in eight different areas, each established with slightly different cultivation methods and seed mixes. The gathered data will eventually be compiled and available to regional horticultural societies, county extension agencies, and the region's schools, in a prime example of the firm's efforts to generate biological information that can be shared.

For NBW, this study has been an education in the creation, monitoring, and maintenance of meadows that can be applied to many other projects. For example, the controlled burning of a meadow every two to three years is essential to fight back invasive grasses, replicating the natural process of fire in local meadows. The exercise is carefully coordinated with fire officials, who judge on the day of the burn if the ground moisture and wind levels are safe for this activity. For twelve years, the meadow burns have continued with great success.

In addition, a program has been developed to control erosion along the course of incised streams, some of which had dropped six feet from their previous levels. Overall, the aim is to repair the damage wreaked by outmoded farming practices and restore horticultural diversity by replanting pond edges and streams with native marginal species.

Two distinct watersheds form the hydrology of the site. The east watershed features a ten-foot-deep, two-and-a-half-acre pond with sinuous edges that is home to larger fish. The west watershed contains a series of shallow stream pools that are retained by check dams and create a home for amphibious species.

Thematic precincts help to guide plant and material choices for the different areas of the landscape and the gardens near the residence. A circular path with a 365-foot radius forms the outer boundary of four garden precincts. A farm-themed area containing a stable and various equipment sheds is planted with red cedars, lindens, maples, and American chestnuts. A pastoral precinct contains expansive meadows,

PRIMARY MATERIALS

Bluestone

Carved granite spillways

Cast-bronze fence and scuppers

Fieldstone

PLANTS

Aesculus parviflora (bottlebrush buckeye)

Andropogon gerardii (big bluestem)

Carpinus caroliniana (American hornbeam)

Carya glabra (pignut hickory)

Castanea dentata (American chestnut)

Cladrastis kentukea (Kentucky yellowwood)

Ginkgo biloba

Gymnocladus dioicus (Kentucky coffeetree)

Juglans nigra (Eastern black walnut)

Juniperus virginiana (Eastern red cedar)

Nyssa sylvatica (black gum)

Quercus alba (white oak)

Quercus falcata (Southern red oak)

Schizachyrium scoparium (little bluestem)

Taxodium distichum (bald cypress)

Ulmus americana 'Princeton' ('Princeton' American elm)

The multiple scales of garden rooms move from intimate terraces and courts adjacent to the residence to large perennial and vegetable gardens in the middle ground and sweeping meadows and woodlands beyond.

hiking trails, streams, and ponds. The wild section features plants endemic to Virginia and the Piedmont region. The garden precinct closest to the house is the most structured, inspired by Virginia's rich history of garden design. Extensive fountains flank a swimming pool near perennial borders, a peony garden, a bowling green, a hedge maze, and a kitchen garden. Near the house, an arced wall radiates from the center of an outdoor dining table that doubles as a sundial. A sunken pollinator garden is filled with plants attractive to hummingbirds, moths, and bats. Around the pool, a series of fountains begins as a trickle from bronze scuppers that fall to basins of pebbles. Granite spillways then send the water in sheets into a long canal, enacting in miniature the narrative of the Piedmont springs that feed its streams, which in turn develop into rivers.

For NBW, this extended project has been the birthplace of many of their most formative and innovative ideas about restoration ecology. Regular monthly meetings with the client over a decade and a half renew their shared commitment to bringing the programs of meadow, forest, and garden into a sustainable balance that continually benefits all.

Top:
A painterly composition of ponds, roads, fencelines, meadows, and individual trees exemplifies the elegant balance of artifice and nature that can be found in agricultural regions.

Bottom:
Slopes surrounding a pond are planted with native marginal species and offer further critical habitat for invertebrates and amphibians.

Opposite top:
A vine-covered pergola atop a dam gives a shady prospect across a fishing pier to a two-acre pond.

Opposite bottom:
Seven Ponds Farm master plan

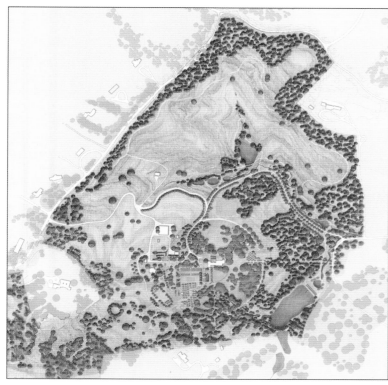

Top:
Massive drifts of individual plant species create dramatic moments along the entry drive.

Bottom left:
A tree swing hangs from the highest branches of a hickory tree. In the distance a hot-air balloon explores the region in the early hours of the day.

Bottom right:
Native red cedar trunks stripped of their bark create a dramatic threshold to the property's Asiatic dell. A series of bridges and boardwalks leads through a woodland garden juxtaposing native plants from America and Japan that share similar growing requirements.

Opposite:
An exuberant garden for pollinators sustains bees throughout the growing season. A clipped gateway of *Viburnum pragensis* hedge leads from the more formal gardens to woodland gardens beyond.

Top:
Views from the house through surrounding gardens emphasize the link between architecture and the landscape.

Bottom:
An elliptical pecan orchard takes its design from a former riding ring and acts as a serene threshold between formal gardens and the wilder native meadows beyond.

Opposite:
Espaliered Asian pears line the walls of a cobbled parking court designed by NBW.

Top:
A long, arcing fieldstone wall creates a plinth for the house that bounds the lawn and highlights views into the woods beyond. The hand-forged bronze rail in the foreground was made by casting branches from the property, using the lost-wax process.

Bottom left:
Custom bronze scuppers animate the fieldstone wall above the swimming pool, evoking European gardens.

Bottom right:
Long granite slabs reclaimed from a demolished building link a nuttery to formal gardens.

Opposite:
A small formal herb garden at the entry to the kitchen is a handy source for a range of edible plants.

Top left:
The swimming pool is framed by fieldstone walls, lines of trees, and clipped hedges combining playfulness and formality.

Top right:
Virginia creeper grows across the facade of the pool pavilion, allowing it to merge with the surrounding gardens.

Bottom left:
The granite troughs of lower walls align with the scuppers of an upper wall, forming a water-informed narrative that runs throughout the various garden rooms.

Bottom right:
Carved granite spillways bring sounds and movement to an eighty-foot-long trough tucked into the retaining wall of the swimming pool.

Opposite:
The NBW-designed pool pavilion offers a trellised loggia for shade and a small changing room and shower for guests. The structure's clean lines and balanced proportions bridge the contemporary garden and the Georgian-style residence beyond.

Top left:
The native meadow is carefully burned in ten-foot-wide bands, with close attention given to prevailing winds to keep the fire under control.

Top right:
Conservation workers can plant up to two thousand trees a day. Waxed tubes provide critical protection from voles, mice, and deer during the establishment period of reforestation projects along the perimeter of the farm.

Bottom:
Tall stands of native grasses and shrubs provide stable slopes, water filtration, and protective wildlife habitat along the borders of the seven ponds.

Opposite:
Large acreages of warm-season native grasses can be maintained by burning every one to two years, eliminating mowing altogether. Fire nourishes the native grasses and helps eliminate non-native fescue and invasive saplings.

Overleaf:
Groves of planted deciduous native trees create an interconnected forest network for wildlife traveling throughout the property. This reforestation work furthers the vision of the extensive master plan.

Orongo Station

Location: North Island, New Zealand
Site area: 3,000 acres
Project dates: 2002–2012

In 1769 Captain James Cook, while discovering what Europeans would later call New Zealand, caught sight of a peninsula on the North Island's rugged coastline. Today, that same dramatic landscape is a vast sheep and cattle station, acquired in 2002 by American clients who hired NBW to set in motion a bold, decade-long design effort. Sustainable agricultural practices would be beautifully interwoven with extensive restoration ecology for threatened flora and fauna—all connected by the powerful thread of the location's historic narrative. To date the most ambitious project of the firm's conservation agriculture studio, this project has become a leading example for sustainable farming in New Zealand.

During their site research, the firm learned that the area's natural ecology had once been temperate rainforest, before decades of standard agricultural and grazing practices eradicated the original woodland and its accompanying seaside wetlands. In order to restore biodiversity to the property, the landscape architects researched those native ecological systems and at the same time worked very closely with a highly involved and visionary property manager to identify which landholdings of the property's three thousand acres could be retired from active farming and grazing. About four hundred acres, or thirteen percent of the farm, were restored to meadow, wetlands, and forest, in the hope that the former populations of invertebrates, birds, and reptiles would return. NBW built a team of ornithologists, conservation biologists, and regional experts to gather information and recommend goals that realistically could be accomplished. Meanwhile, in the midst of this deluge of information, the firm never lost sight of their primary role of creating form through interpreting the huge amount of ecological data related to the vast site, while at the same time designing a series of domestically scaled gardens around the client's historic home that could represent in microcosm their mission for the greater landscape.

Along seven miles of Pacific coastline, the steeply sloping hills had never been suitable for crop farming because of their sharp grade, and therefore had been used exclusively for grazing sheep. These beautiful but barren slopes needed to be reforested to protect the topography from frequent slips and mini-landslides that send sediment into the Pacific Ocean below.

Ornithologists and biologists advised the firm on the grades and elevations required for various avian species to nest and feed on newly formed wetland islands, which restored sixty-four acres of original wetlands that previously had been drained for cattle grazing. The result was a boldly graphic design of arced water bodies, streams, channels, and islands that drain water from several hundred acres. The desire was not to replicate nature but to use scientific data as a basis for artful landscape architecture, constructing a functioning wetland that—while clearly a work of artifice rather than nature—provides vital ecological services to the region.

PRIMARY MATERIALS

Cast-concrete feeding trough
Regional limestone
Repurposed timber rafters for bridge
Stuccoed concrete walls

PLANTS

Cordyline australis (cabbage tree or ti kouka)

Corynocarpus laevigatus (karaka)

Cyathea medullaris (black tree fern or mamaku)

Dacrydium cupressinum (rimu)

Hebe spp. (koromiko)

Hoheria populnea (lacebark)

Leptospermum scoparium (tea tree or manuka)

Metrosideros excelsa (New Zealand Christmas tree or pohutukawa)

Myoporum debile (ngaio)

Phormium cookianum (mountain flax or wharariki)

Phormium tenax (giant flax or harakeke)

Pittosporum crassifolium (karo)

Podocarpus totara (totara)

Rhopalostylis sapida (nikau)

Sophora tetraphylla (kowhai)

Vitex lucens (puriri)

Distinctive one-foot-wide terraces formed by herds of sheep walking parallel to the hilly New Zealand topography accommodate the planting of reforestation trees on otherwise dramatically steep hillsides.

The constant threat of invasive exotic mammals (the island lacks any endemic mammal species save two species of bat) is one of the largest challenges to bird and plant life at this site and throughout New Zealand. The firm commissioned an eight-foot-high steel fence along one perimeter as a barrier against exotic animals such as European possums, rats, weasels, stoats, and cats. On the other sides of the peninsula, precipitous white cliffs form a natural barrier. After the area was cleared, the landscape architects initiated a lengthy collaboration with conservation biologists and horticulturists to attract endangered and threatened bird and reptile species such as the sooty petrel (a native bird) and the endangered tuatara (the two species of which are the only surviving members of an order of reptile distinct from lizard and snakes, and which lives in a symbiotic relationship with the nesting birds). Throughout, the aim has been to rebuild a native ecology while consulting with local experts as well as Maori officials, since certain features of the land are sacred to their culture. Consistent effort has been made to bring greater visibility to the earthworks related to the habitations, food supplies, and fortifications of the previous Maori inhabitants.

In an unfamiliar ecology, where because of its isolation most native species are endemic, NBW strives to conduct a program that is tailor-made for the site, but which doesn't vary in principle from the core concepts reflected in each and every one of the firm's projects. They always start with research into a site: its cultural history, topography, and ecological history. From these excavations they build a narrative that informs all the design, plant, and material choices for the project, transforming the site into a sustainable and highly contemporary work of art.

Top:
Seven miles of coastal cliffs are planned as critical wildlife corridors; replanted native temperate rain-forest trees aid in stabilizing steep clay slopes that are dangerously prone to landslides.

Bottom:
A fence delineates the stark difference between successfully reforested wildlife enclosure and paddocks that continue to be grazed by livestock.

Opposite top:
NBW installed a predator-proof fence that prevents aggressive mammals from entering the enclosure, protecting newly re-established communities of native birds, reptiles, and invertebrates from imported invaders.

Opposite bottom:
Orongo Station master plan

Top:
An S-curve earthen dam separates saltwater wetland from freshwater ponds, thereby creating a greater diversity of habitats for plants and animals. Mown paths allow visitors to hike through the wetlands to view the remarkable biodiversity of this habitat up close..

Bottom:
A view across newly constructed wetlands reveals freshwater treatment ponds to the right, a saltwater marsh in the center, and a freshwater wetland that forms a connection for wildlife to the Fero-Fero Lagoon in the distance.

Opposite:
Sloping islands within the seventy-five acres of designed wetlands were graded and planted to accommodate the specific needs of threatened and endangered migratory birds.

Overleaf:
A farm access road and shelter belts of trees were designed to focus awareness on the historic Ngāti Manuhiri cemetery mounds in the distance. This is one of many examples where the artifacts of previous inhabitants and other cultures have been central to the focus of contemporary programmatic needs.

Top:
Low walls and hedges delineate outdoor rooms close to the house. A large outdoor fireplace and chimney anchor a garden used for outdoor dining. The restoration of temperate rain forest can be seen in the distance.

Bottom:
A simple vocabulary of masonry walls, sheared hedges, and loose perennials strikes a balance between clipped formal shapes and wilder forms and textures in the Homestead Garden.

Opposite:
Garage and gym buildings were designed by NBW as contemporary interpretations of regional farm buildings and sheds incorporating wood slats and corrugated steel. Water from the roofs falls into large scuppers and is captured for domestic use in large cisterns.

Top:
A narrow lap pool is tucked between two buildings, surrounded by a collection of native tree ferns that creates a primordial and mysterious sense of retreat.

Bottom:
The outdoor fireplace, clipped hedges, and canopy trees form an intimate outdoor room for entertaining.

Opposite:
An aerial view of the historic residence and guesthouse shows rain-forest restoration in the foreground and the Earthworks Garden in the distance.

Top:
The layout of the citrus paddocks is oriented around an axis leading to the historic Maori cemetery (or *urupa*) in the distance.

Bottom:
The Earthworks Garden's carefully constructed terraces and mounds were inspired by traditional Maori landform construction.

Opposite:
A narrow garden walk lined with spheres of native hebes leads guests from the Homestead Garden to the Endeavor Garden and ultimately to the Earthworks Garden, with dramatic views of the coastal mountain range in the distance.

Overleaf:
The Earthworks Garden borrows both views and its inspiration from terraced hills in the distance. The sweeping planting is composed of several varieties of hebe to provide a variety of texture and blooms over a long season.

Medlock Ames

Location: Sonoma, California
Site area: 1 acre
Project dates: 2009–2011

This project represents the first phase of NBW's master plan for a 360-acre biodynamic vineyard. The former general store and its small pleasure and edible garden make a compelling case for the aesthetic possibilities of sustainable practices on a domestic scale and permit the owners of the vineyard—located five miles away—to showcase their cultivation practices and their processes for agricultural and wildlife conservation.

The firm began by removing an asphalt parking lot surrounding the store and converting it into an outdoor gathering space with tables on terraces of decomposed granite. Visitors can sample wine under olive trees surrounded by raised beds of vegetables and herbs. The conversion from pavement to garden is a simple act that can easily be replicated in urban settings where asphalt or concrete slab reigns supreme.

One of the most revolutionary concepts of the design is its foregrounding of stormwater management. A network of raingardens and swales planted with native rushes becomes the primary feature of the garden, turning a previously impermeable site into one that retains its runoff; this is a small-scale representation of one of the essential ideas of the Medlock Ames vineyard's design. Small informational signs explain the vineyard's stormwater system and cultivation techniques. It's a subtle, pleasantly didactic element that can be engaged with or overlooked depending on whether a visitor is interested in the teaching aspects of the space or enjoying it as pleasure garden.

Groves of decades-old olive trees, refugees of changing agricultural practices in the valley, were moved to the garden to lend a suitably Mediterranean atmosphere and much-needed shade. They punctuate the ground in lines that echo the rows of grapes in the surrounding fields or in symmetrical groups that preside over mini-meadows of native grasses and bulbs. Raised beds of galvanized steel reminiscent of water tanks and feeding troughs are filled with organically grown vegetables and herbs that emphasize the region's strong historic love of food and wine. The elements of the small space are designed to unite the long-standing agricultural traditions of the valley as a laboratory of sustainable concepts with the Bay Area's reputation as one of the nation's foremost culinary destinations.

PRIMARY MATERIALS

Board-formed concrete

Decomposed granite

Galvanized-steel raised beds

Repurposed western red cedar siding used in fencing

Stripped cedar posts

PLANTS

Arctostaphylos manzanita 'Dr. Hurd' ('Dr. Hurd' manzanita)

Calamagrostis foliosa (leafy reed grass)

Eschscholzia californica ssp. *maritima* (California poppy)

Euphorbia characias ssp. *wulfenii* (milkwort)

Feijoa sellowiana (strawberry guava)

Festuca mairei (Atlas fescue)

Festuca rubra 'Molate' (California red fescue)

Juncus patens (California gray rush)

Lupinus arboreus (yellow bush lupine)

Mimulus cardinalis (scarlet monkeyflower)

Muhlenbergia rigens (California deergrass)

Olea europaea 'Ascolano' ('Ascolano' olive)

Olea europaea 'Little Ollie' (dwarf olive)

Platanus racemosa (California sycamore)

Quercus lobata (valley oak)

At Medlock Ames, grass-filled swales and a bioretention garden filter stormwater and educate visitors about water usage and sustainability.

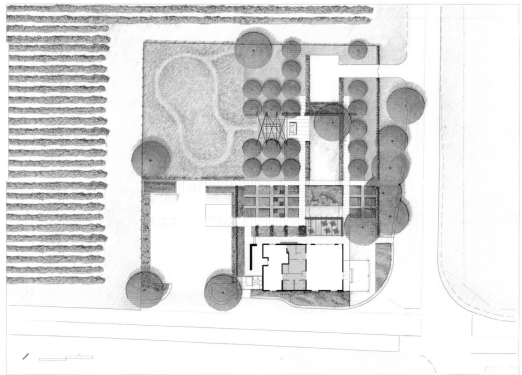

Top:
Triple-sash windows can be opened to become doors between a tasting room and a terrace overlooking the gardens and vineyards beyond.

Bottom:
Plan of Medlock Ames

Opposite:
Paths made of concrete pavers cast on site lead visitors among raised vegetable and herb beds, an olive grove, and gathering spaces. A fence in the foreground is made of new steel frames supporting repurposed wood siding from old farm buildings found on the site.

Overleaf:
Herbs are cultivated in great variety for pairings in wine tasting. Two rows of juncus rush indicate stormwater conveyance swales for the flat site.

Top:
Rather than hide stormwater infrastructure around the periphery, NBW designed a raingarden to occupy a central location, spotlighting the course of water through the site.

Bottom:
A grid of metal planters and plant towers designed by NBW interspersed with crushed stone paths brings order to abundant plantings.

Opposite:
The level tops of the custom-designed planters of galvanized steel reveal the slight slope of the site.

Top:
An outdoor fire pit and other seating areas are enclosed by board-formed concrete walls and a mature olive grove that was transplanted to the site. NBW designed a long picnic table that features a metal trough in its center for ice and chilled wine.

Bottom:
Simple strings of white carnival lights strung from stripped cedar poles create a playful yet romantic evening atmosphere.

Opposite:
Multiple forms of stormwater conveyance determined the design of the garden's social spaces. Rain chains, planted channels, and swales throughout the site amplify the theme of water management for the visitor.

Overleaf:
The agriculturally inspired geometry of the tasting-room garden packs a strong educational program into a small space while maintaining visual appeal and a sense of plantsmanship.

WORKBOOK

WATER

1
A bronze scupper set in a fieldstone wall evokes hand pumps found on early Virginia farms.

2
A small plunge pool creates a mirror to the sky.

3
Stormwater treatment is central to a corporate campus offering meditation areas and running trails.

4
Canals and dikes function as a highly aesthetic stormwater-treatment water garden.

Water is integral to many of NBW's landscape designs. A site's hydrologic patterns can animate and enliven an outdoor space. Water provides movement, light reflection, and sound in a manner that seems intrinsic—never imposed or false. Humans find the play, movement, and mere presence of water mesmerizing.

Water's role may be expressed as simply as the flow from a spout into a basin; on a larger scale, the course of an entire stream or river may be remediated or altered to prevent erosion. A comprehensive understanding of a landscape's variations in rainfall, flooding, and drought is gained from extensive research and a series of site visits during different seasons. The fundamental patterns that emerge over time reveal the long history of a site, stretching from prehuman times to the modern day and informing a water-based narrative that determines design cues for an entire project.

5
A chain of ponds slows stormwater and establishes a habitat for insects and amphibians in the middle of twenty acres of restored warm-season grass meadows.

6
A wooden fishing bridge provides access to a small island covered in native marginal grasses and perennials.

7
A grass stage and its surrounding water gardens are the focus of a botanic garden's amphitheater.

8
Scuppers surrounding the stage link the upper and lower basins and provide a constant sound of splashing water.

9
A zero-waterline edge links a swimming pool seamlessly to Jamaica's Montego Bay, visible in the distance.

10
Historic stone cisterns found on the island of Jamaica inspire a swimming pool. A cut-stone deck surrounds a glass-tile-lined pool with a remarkable clarity.

11
A curvilinear pool in New Zealand is surrounded by native plants and expansive views to the ocean in the distance.

12
Wide spillways circulate water in shallow dipping pools designed for children.

13
Cardinal flower (*Lobelia cardinalis*) and Needlerush (*Juncus effusus*) are the primary plants in the street-side raingardens at Citygarden. A metal-grating bridge allows stormwater to pass from one side of the sidewalk to the other.

14
A reflecting pool above the waterfall in Citygarden offers a seamless view of the monumental sculpture beyond.

15
A bioretention garden collects stormwater runoff from the parking lot next to it, establishing habitat for wildlife and seasonal interest from colorful native plants.

16.
Water overflows from a swimming pool to a shallow children's plunge pool below.

17
A small dipping pool in a bluestone terrace overlooks meadows and hills.

18
The stormwater treatment meadow of flowering plants and grasses at Citygarden accommodates runoff from nearby hard surfaces. Behind it, a waterfall evokes the tributaries of the Mississippi.

19
A pebble-filled rill highlights the connection between two water features.

20
A series of water features, each increasing in size and scale, leads the eye down an important axis at a Long Island estate.

21
Evoking the meandering forms of the waterways of Tidewater Virginia, a lap pool is enclosed but separate from a larger freshwater pool.

22
Simple bronze pipes circulate water in a New Zealand swimming pool. A wall of parged stone is inspired by historic cisterns found in the region.

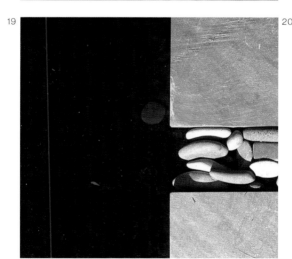

23
A swimming pool in Long Island is surrounded by native flowering plants and functions as the heart of a family retreat.

24
Flat panels of grass flank a dark plaster swimming pool, creating gathering areas for family and guests.

25
A stone wall embedded with boulders evokes the Fall Line of Northern Virginia while animating and aerating sheets of falling water.

26
A placid pool of water that gathers roof runoff from the site's surrounding buildings reflects a sculptural mature live oak.

27
A granite fountain basin and spillway align perfectly with a distant mountain peak.

28
In this lap pool, swimmers find themselves in close proximity to wildlife and wetland plants. A wall separates the pool water from adjacent stormwater.

23

24

25

26

27

28

29
The calm surface of this swimming pool reflects both tree trunks and building columns to inventive effect.

30
A swimming pool slips beneath a mature canopy of live oaks and visually connects to a freshwater pond beyond.

31
Smooth pavers contrast with rugged natural stone to enclose a rectangular water feature.

32
A stream falls through a stone channel, over a pair of sandstone walls, and down into a plunge pool.

33
Oversized metal rain chains direct rainwater from a roof to a catch basin below.

34
A concrete meander fountain is the point of origin for a rill leading to a garden pool.

PLANTS

1
Native wildflowers and grasses planted in large drifts that resemble the site's surrounding meadows fill the forecourt of a private residence.

2
In New Zealand kahikatea trees are planted inside protective wire cages in an arc around a historic Maori cemetery. Eventually the saplings will grow to ninety feet tall, encircling the burial mounds like sentinels.

3
Paths mown through warm-season grasses provide access and reveal the spatial qualities of the meadow.

4
An allée of amelanchier trees gives structure to a walkway between a former dairy barn and a tiny cheese-processing building. NBW designed the restoration of both buildings.

Many of NBW's landscapes emphasize a sense of regeneration. Well-chosen plants are a primary method for weaving a site damaged from construction or neglect back into its setting. Native plants create valuable links between the work of the designer and site, but they are only part of the story. Man's interaction with plant species—horticultural and agricultural, native and imported—inform the firm's selection of species as much as attention to the naturally occurring foliage of a setting. These all-important cultural factors, including human settlement patterns and economics, combine with environmental considerations such as animal migratory routes and climate to make a place a place. Contextualization is key. Careful attention to soil type and microbiology in selecting plants—whether endemic or exotic—creates living site-specific installations that will thrive without undue maintenance or coddling.

1

2

3

4

5
In autumn, the vivid seedheads of *Muhlenbergia capillaris* (pink muhly grass) create a colorful display.

6
A line of *Taxodium distichum* (bald cypress) in brilliant fall color mark the edge of a pond.

7
A plant-filled raingarden marks the arrival point of a small garden while conveying the client's commitment to sustainability.

8
Ferns and other shade-loving plants evoke the feeling of wild woodland in the highly urban setting of a small city courtyard.

9
A carved limestone tank surrounded by vegetable plants serves as a cold-water dipping pool next to a cedar-lined sauna.

10
The sauna's entry garden is planted with a wide variety of edible plants.

11
Fast-growing hops wind up steel cables to cloak a garden wall in an urban courtyard.

12
A lawn terrace leads to a bluestone path flanked with overflowing clumps of lady's mantle.

13
Existing brick walls cloaked in jasmine frame an English perennial border in a sculpture garden in Italy.

14
Stone walls topped with large granite urns designed by NBW are ensconced in the lush foliage of native plants.

15
Rudbeckia and echinacea form long-lasting displays of bright midsummer color.

16
An arc of arborvitae creates a backdrop to perennial terraces in a Long Island garden.

17
Myrica pensylvanica, a coastal shrub native to eastern North America, is sheared into hedges that follow the slopes of walls and ramps in a formal garden area.

18
The dramatic texture and colors of native wildflowers stand out against the backdrop of a board-formed concrete wall.

19
A wooden stair accesses trails through a restoration planting of lush native temperate rain forest in New Zealand.

20
The front door of a residence is flanked by a line of multistemmed *Betula nigra*.

21
A sinuous driveway is intentionally encroached upon by close woodland plantings of ferns, *Cercis canadensis*, and *Amelanchier canadensis*.

22
Large, near wild-looking drifts of ferns, native shrubs, and perennials flank a curving section of a circular path in a woodland garden.

23
A highly stylized planting of native hebes emphasizes the strong geometry of an earthwork in New Zealand.

24
A grove of multistemmed crape myrtles, chosen for their sculptural qualities and warm bark color, catch the light of the setting sun.

25
The plant species for this garden were selected to attract a diversity of pollinators, including the honey bees strategically located on the opposite side of the vegetable garden.

26
The strong geometry of sheared evergreens punctuates looser beds of flowering perennials and a large purple smokebush at a Long Island estate.

27
Native wildflowers mixed with warm-season grasses in a Connecticut meadow attract wildlife and important pollinators.

28
Muhlenbergia capillaris (pink muhly grass) in full colorful bloom surrounds a bench along a wetland path at WaterColor in the Florida Panhandle.

29
The perennial gardens on the raised terraces surrounding a Connecticut house feature cultivars of the same native wildflowers found in a restored meadow below.

30
Ferns fill the bottom of a silo adjacent to a refurbished dairy barn.

31
Espaliered pears line a walled parking court, providing flower, fruit, and beautiful winter structure.

32
The intricately peeling bark texture of these river birches was an important consideration in placing these trees near a raised walkway.

33
A cutting garden sited in front of a potting shed designed by NBW supplies fresh flowers for the homeowners.

34
Peach blossoms create a vivid contrast to the strong winter color of little bluestem grass.

STONE AND WOOD

1
Fieldstone piers are topped with sandstone slabs to form benches along a terrace overlook.

2
Large piers of Shenandoah fieldstone mark the thresholds of a series of courts and garden rooms. A reclaimed granite cobble street was repurposed to make a motor court.

3
Regional stone creates a sense of cohesion at the arrival court of a New Zealand lodge.

4
NBW designed an eighteen-foot-tall custom steel gabion to be filled with boulders. Light shines through the gaps between the stones.

The goal of each new project is to delve deep below surface aesthetics. Naturally, color, finish, and texture are all factors. However, as a design progresses, larger concepts become increasingly important in building compelling narratives. Broad influences such as a site's regional geology and natural history inform choices of building materials, which can be positioned in the landscape to reference nearby geologic features. The study of ancient glacial movements can determine how the stone is shaped and sited, connecting a project to its surroundings. In addition to geologic processes, NBW explores man's long-standing relationship with both stone and wood, highlighting regional traditions and venerable methods of quarrying and carpentry, further exploring how to root each project meaningfully within its context.

5
Stone paving, walls, piers, and benches celebrate the art of the stoneworkers who created them.

6
A crushed-stone motor court allows plants to grow through the medium while permitting water infiltration during heavy rain.

7
A tall fieldstone chimney anchors the outdoor dining area of a garden terrace.

8
Thin bluestone is set vertically on its side in stone dust to construct an intricate herringbone pattern.

9
Arced bands of crisp masonry form the seating of a grass-covered memorial amphitheater.

10
A sixteen-foot-long white marble bench designed by NBW responded to the geometry of existing stone paving in a sculpture garden.

11
Shenandoah fieldstone fills steel-wire gabion baskets, giving structure to walls while permitting stormwater infiltration.

12
Irregular bluestone pavers are embedded in groundcover plants, eliminating the need for frequently mown lawn.

13
Bluestone slabs carefully fitted into fieldstone walls create integral benches.

14
Concrete and local stone walls give an impressive, almost ceremonial structure to the forecourt of a New Zealand lodge. A staircase leads up through a planted native-grass meadow in the distance.

15
A simple board-formed concrete basin calls to mind livestock watering troughs. Bronze pipes supply the return water to a circulating fountain.

16
An elliptical fieldstone wall creates the sense of a clearing within a native shrub garden.

17
Massive blocks of roughly carved limestone
form piers that anchor fieldstone walls
surrounding a swimming pool.

18
The unusual angle of stone stairs brings
a dynamic tension to this garden room.

19
Stone retaining walls create a series of
grassy ramps, establishing an accessible
route through a terraced garden.

20
Crushed stone fills Cor-Ten steel bands to
create steps in a terraced vegetable garden.

21
Board-formed concrete walls and pavers
were cast on site in a California garden.

22
Fieldstone walls establish a frame
of plinth-like structures for a coastal
perennial garden.

23
A wide variety of stone finishes covers tall piers at a garden for a stone company.

24
Low walls double as seats for larger gatherings in a perennial garden.

25
A highly polished granite seat wall swoops dramatically around a rough-cut limestone wall.

26
An ellipse of bluestone and lawn gracefully marks an important intersection in a formal garden.

27
Patterns of basalt contrast with the veining of sandstone, bringing a rich texture to terraces planted with grasses.

28
Each capstone of a wall is selected and placed to reveal its most visually interesting side.

23

24

25

26

27

28

29
A low arc wall of fieldstone caps a perennial garden and establishes a boundary between the formal and informal portions of a garden.

30
Vines are beginning to cover the piers and eventually will grow over the trellis of a pergola to provide vital midsummer shade.

31
Curved stone-slab steps lead to a sinuous crushed-stone walk in the distance.

32
Board-formed concrete walls frame a series of terraced beds of loosely growing perennials in a small urban garden.

33
Limestone stepping stones made of locally quarried stone cross a reflecting pool and offer entertainment for children and adults.

34
Stone piers form structural abutments for a wooden bridge at the entry to a cattle farm.

Credits

Carnegie Hill House
Client private; **NBW team** Thomas Woltz, Dorothy Bothwell, Jennifer Brooks, Christina Michas; **Structural engineer** Gilsanz Murray Steficek; **Contractor** Plant Specialists: Paul Harness; **Carpenter** Ivory Build: Anthony Visco

The Cedars
Client private; **NBW team** Thomas Woltz, Mary Williams Wolf, Sophie Johnston, Anne Pray, Kathy Kambic, Beth Kaleida, Christina Michas, Sara Osborne; **Architect** Cicognani Kalla Architects: Nicholas Stanos, Ann Kalla; **Civil engineer** VHB Engineering; **Electrician** Ronkonkoma Electric; **Surveyor** Jerry La Rue; **Lighting designer** Maggie Guisto, Pat McGillicuddy; **Contractor** Roy Anderson Associates; **Masonry** John O'Connell; **Irrigation contractor** MDS Equipment Co; **Landscape contractor** Whitmore's Landscaping; **Tree care and removal** Wonderland Tree Care; **Pool contractor** Gibbons Pools; **Wood fencing and gates** Walpole Woodworkers; **Tennis court** Tennis Planning Corp; **Wood entrance gates and cabinets** Fairfield Woodworks; **Steel fabricator** Tebbens Steel

Iron Mountain House
Client private; **NBW team** Thomas Woltz, Jeffrey Longhenry, Dorothy Bothwell, Jennifer Brooks, Jennifer Horn; **Meadow consultant** Larry Weaner Landscape Associates; **Plant consultant** Rosedale Nursery; **General contractor** Structure Works

Asia Trail at the National Zoo
Client The Smithsonian Institution; **NBW team** Warren T. Byrd Jr., Mary Williams Wolf, Sara Coates Myhre, Hara Wilkiemeyer, Evan Grimm, Sophie Johnston, Matt Whitaker, Eugene Ryang, Breck Gastinger, Emmanuel Didier, Michael Stouse; **Architect (prime)** Chatelain Architects: Leon Chatelain, Stuart Billings, Jon Penndorf; **MEP** Ove Arup & Partners: Adam Trojanowski, Elizabeth Perez, Julian Astbury, Leroy Le-Lacheur; **Structural engineer** McMullan & Associates: Doug Bond, Colleen Nasta; **Civil engineer** William H. Gordon Associates: Scott Peterson, Laura Miller; **Exhibits** Smithsonian National Zoological Park Exhibits Department: Susan Ades, Kara Blond, Ken Stuart; **Rockwork designer and habitat consultant** Rampantly Creative (now called Coyle & Caron): Quentin Caron, Sally Coyle; **Rockwork engineer/cable-structure engineer** Weidlinger Associates: Peter Quigley, Assaad El-Haddad; **Trail-lighting designer** D. Gilmore Lighting Design: Debra Gilmore, Gaspar Glusberg; **Animal pool and stream engineer** Siska-Aurand: Doug Aurand; **Irrigation designer** Irrigation Research: Bill Rogers; **Art director for rockwork and habitat construction** Karen Phillips (now called Habitat Design Studio); **General contractor** Hensel Phelps Construction Co.; **Construction manager** Bovis Lend Lease/Smithsonian; **Smithsonian Institution construction** Marc Muller, Karen Swanson; **Rockwork construction** Cemrock; **Landscape contractor** Ruppert Nurseries

Flight 93 National Memorial
Client National Park Service: Joann Hanley, Keith Newlin, Jeff Reinbold, Jodie Petersen; **NBW team** Warren T. Byrd Jr., Todd Shallenberger, Breck Gastinger, Emmanuel Didier, Jeremy Jordan, Evan Grimm, Matt Whitaker, Mike Smith, Tommy Solomon, Paul Josey, Jennifer Trompetter; **Architect (prime)** Paul Murdoch Architects; **Civil engineer/surveyor** The EADS Group; **Civil engineer/**

MEP/fire protection H. F. Lenz Company; **Structural engineer** Robert Silman Associates; **Lighting** George Sexton & Associates; **Soil and water testing** Biohabitats; **Wetland delineation** Louis Berger Group; **Cost estimator** Davis Langdon; **General contractor** Arrow Kinsley Joint Venture; **Construction supervisor** US Army Corps of Engineers; **Planting contractor, Phase 1A** Arrow Walace Pancher; **Road planting contractor** Davey Resource Group and Vanasse Hangen Brustlin; **Grove planting contractor** Biohabitats

Citygarden
Client The Gateway Foundation; **NBW team** Warren T. Byrd Jr., Sara Coates Myhre, Mary Williams Wolf, Breck Gastinger, Paul Josey, Jeremy Jordan, Evan Grimm; **Owner's representative** Arcturis: Sara Runge; **Architect for Terrace View Café and maintenance building** Studio | Durham Architects: Phil Durham, Greg Worley, Darci Thomas; **Structural engineer** Frontenac Engineering Group: Mohamed T. Al Harash; **Civil engineer** Frontenac Engineering Group: Steve Miller; **MEP** Ross & Baruzzini: Paul E. Carmen Sr.; **Sculpture structural engineer** Larson Engineering: Ted Pruess, Marie Newman; **Fountains** Hydro Dramatics: Anne Gunn, Kerry Friedman, Dan Heinlein, Shawn Boyd; **Site lighting** Fisher Marantz Stone: Charles Stone, Zack Zanolli, Rebecca Ho-Dion; **Sculpture lighting** Randy Burkett Lighting Design: Randy Burkett, Susan Jennings; **Sculpture installation** Acme Erectors: Aron Clay; **Visual communication** Bliss Collaborative: Pam Bliss, Kathleen Robert; **Communication strategy and information design** Act 3 Studio: Ben Kaplan; **Irrigation** Irrigation Research Management: Steve Niehoff; **Soils** Jeffrey L. Bruce & Co.: Jeffrey Bruce, David Stokes, Eric Becker; **Plant consultant** Missouri Botanical Garden: June Hutson, Jim Cocos; **Cost estimator** Everest Estimating Services: Rich Ullrich; **General contractor** BSI Constructors: Paul McLeane, Doug Hawkins, Joseph Kaiser, Dan Kloeppel; **Subcontractors** Cold Spring Granite, Daktronics, DKW Construction Co., Earthworks, Engraphix Architectural Signage, Environmental Design/Instant Shade Tree, Franklin Mechanical, Kaiser Electric, Kirkwood Masonry, Landesign, Leonard Masonry

Campbell Hall at the University of Virginia
Client University of Virginia, Charlottesville, Virginia; **UVA School of Architecture** Karen Van Lengen; **UVA Facilities Planning and Construction** Steve Ratliff; **NBW team** Warren T. Byrd Jr., Todd Shallenberger, Serena Nelson, Sara Osborne, Robin Carmichael, Emmanuel Didier, Michael Stouse; **Design architect, East Pavilion addition** W. G. Clark Associates; **Design architect, South Wing addition** William Sherman; **Architect of record** SMBW Architects; **Structural engineer** Fox & Associates; **Civil engineer** Draper Aden Associates; **MEP** Whitescarver, Hurd & Obenchain; **General contractor** Donley's: Mac Donley, Mike Castle; **Concrete fabrication** Cleveland Cement Contractors; **Sitework** Linco; **Stonework** Faulconer Construction; **Planting** Windridge Landscaping Company

The Dell at the University of Virginia
Client University of Virginia, Office of the Architect, Charlottesville, Virginia: Mary V. Hughes; **NBW team** Warren T. Byrd Jr., Kennon Williams, Kent Dougherty, Emmanuel Didier, Robin Carmichael, Jason Kreuzer, Theresa Steward; **Fluvial engineers/hydrologists/ecologists** Biohabitats of Maryland: Tom Burkett, Vince

Sortman; Biohabitats of Virginia: Lee Mallonee; **Civil engineers** Nitsch Engineering: Stephen Benz; PHR&A Engineering: John Reno; **Project management and interface with John Paul Jones Arena project** VMDO Architects: Chris Weatherford

WaterColor
Client The St. Joe Company, Jacksonville, Florida; **NBW team** Warren T. Byrd Jr., Kennon Williams, Thomas L. Woltz, Mary Williams Wolf, Breck Gastinger, Lara Call, Hugh Truslow, Anne Russell, Pete O'Shea, Jason Kreuzer, Jim Kovach, Evan Grimm, Emmanuel Didier, Jeff Aten, Todd Shallenberger, Matt Whitaker, Schaffer Sommers; **Architect** Cooper Robertson & Partners; **Civil engineer** PBS&J; **Contractor** Brasfield Gorrie; **Surveyor** Gulfside Surveying Company

Seven Ponds
Client private; **NBW team** Thomas Woltz, Warren T. Byrd Jr., Breck Gastinger, Jeff Aten, Anne Pray, Jim Kovach, Christina Michas, Hara Wilkiemeyer, Lara Call; **Landscape contractor** Jay Townsend; **Structural engineer** Nolen Frisa, Damon Littlefield; **Granite carving for fountain** Stone Forest; **Pool/fountain consultant** Siska-Aurand: Doug Aurand, Charlottesville Aquatics; **General contractor** Alexander Nicholson; **Bridges/trellises** Jerry Sackett; **Bronze work** Robert Bricker

Orongo Station
Client private; **NBW team** Thomas Woltz, Breck A. Gastinger, Jim Kovach, Evan Grimm, Sara Coates Myhre, Karl Krause, David Timmerman, Hara Wilkiemeyer, Emmanuel Didier, Jeremy Jordan, Jeff Aten, Kathy Kambic, Alissa Diamond; **Design architect** Thomas Woltz; **Architects of record** James Blackburn, Robin Butt; **Interior design** Marianne Mackey Interior Design: Chic Mackey; Katie Ridder Design and Decoration: Katie Ridder; S. R. Gambrel: Steven Gambrel; **Station staff** Kim Dodgshun; Chris Smart; John Williams; Kerry Teutenberg; Troy Teutenberg; Des Mills; Chick Bridge; Dee Hawkins; Ronald Kimber; Peter Ruha; Travis Dalton; David Newlands; Wendy, Jock, and Lily Dodgshun; **The Ngai Tamanuhiri** Ngai Tamanuhiri Whanui Trust: Dawn Pomana, Noel Pohatu; **Ecological services** Ecoworks: Steve Sawyer, Sandy Bull; Native Tree Planters: Tom Stone; **Ngati Porou fencing** Excluder Fence Company: Bert Peachy; Agfirst Engineering: Ian Howatson; **Horticulture consultant** Native Garden Nursery: Nigel and Lana Hope; **Building contractor** Roger Evans; **Surveying** Grant & Cook Surveyors: Murray Harris; **Bridge general contractor:** Bill Ireland; **Structural Engineer:** Phil Gaby; **Landscape contractor** Escape Landscapes: Jeff Bills, Steve Webster

Medlock Ames
Client Medlock Ames Winery, Alexander Valley, California; **NBW team** Thomas Woltz, Jeffrey Longhenry, Dorothy Bothwell, Jennifer Brooks; **Architect of record** Tierney/Figueiredo Architects; **Interior architect** Wade Design Architects; **Interior designer** Wick Design Group; **Local landscape architect** Alexis Woods Landscape Design; **Meadow consultant** Greenlee and Associates; **General contractor** EarthTone Construction: Andy Bannister; **Landscape contractor** Creative Environments

Special thanks to David Lepage at Nelson Byrd Woltz for his production coordination on this book